—— BOOK I: ——
# THE EARLY YEARS

# STRICTLY PRIVATE TO PUBLIC EXPOSURE

*Series 1: A Plateful of Privilege*

## BOOK I:

# THE EARLY YEARS

# ALEXANDER THYNN
## THE MARQUESS OF BATH

**Artnik**
London

© Alexander Thynn, 2002

First published in book form in Great Britain 2002
by Artnik
26 Pont Street
London
SW1X 0AB

ISBN 1 903906 24 5

Design and typeset by Linda Wade

Printed in Bulgaria by DEMAX PLC

# Contents

## PART ONE:
## FAMILY BACKGROUND

# PART FOUR: LUDGROVE (2)

❊

# Foreword

### NIGEL DEMPSTER

Alexander Thynne is flamboyant, controversial, celebrated, decadent and, at least for a journalist, wonderful copy. In fact, he is a gossip columnist's dream: a wealthy peer with a magnificent stately home who aside from holding eccentric views on virtually everything has acquired a staggering number of wifelets. A harem, in fact, that would cause many a 16th century sultan to eat his heart out. Small wonder that for over twenty-five years he has been regular feature in my *Daily Mail* Dairy.

Actually it was me who dubbed him the "the Loins of Longleat", a tag which has sort of stuck. As he is so colourful, he has attracted a great deal of this kind of press coverage. Yet, having read the first three books of his autobiography, *Strictly Private to Public Exposure*, I rather wish I had looked behind his public image. I can now see there a lot more facets to his character than the media concedes.

It is very easy, for example, to assume that as Alexander is unconventional and hedonistic he is also indulgent and dissolute. Nothing, as the barest of facts about his full autobiography prove, could be further from the case. So far, this quite monumental chronicle amounts to over 5 million words! Just to produce them would break the back of most professional scribblers. But they are also well-written and informative. These books are a delight to read. His style is elegant, light and, in the best English tradition, gently ironical. It is a rare page that will not draw a wry smile from the reader.

Moreover, in taking readers through the journey of his life and its antecedents, he effortlessly leaves them with a sense of history, an

1

understanding of what made England. Aside from such unexpected delights, my overriding surprise from reading *The Early Years*, the first book of the trilogy, was to recognise how astonishingly hard-working and disciplined he has been and, even in his seventies, continues to be. For all the drinking, eating and wifelet-ing, which we columnists and diarists like to imagine consumes Alexander at Longleat and in his St Tropez villa, he clearly does not let it interfere with his writing.

Aside from the books, though, Alexander is also a poet, prolific artist, sportsman, politician, polemicist, stately home showman... How he has packed it all in defeats me. Who would have thought, for example, that he was an Eton and Army boxing champion? I think if I had known that my more punchy items on his life might have been rather less hard-hitting. Of course, as those who know him, Alexander is always the perfect English gentleman. He never stands on protocol despite having a bloodline that has a far more aristocratic pedigree than those sticklers for formality, the Windsors. Alexander can be "Your Grace" or "My Lord" as easily as he can be just plain Alexander. I'm sure that the assault on a man in Campden Hill Road in 1994 must have been – as he claims – a case of mistaken identity. But, if it wasn't, well I am sure the bounder deserved all he got.

The picture that Alexander paints of his upbringing in *The Early Years* shows us more elegant, charming, gentler times. Those days will never return and live on only in accounts such as his but reading of them made me feel that the world would be a better place if his era had lasted longer. He does not look back at his life through the rose-tinted glasses of nostalgia but with a warm eye that always lights on what it is valuable to record, remember and celebrate.

Alexander often refers to his many murals that adorn the walls of Longleat – some like the Kama Sutra room with explicitly sexual themes – as "keyhole glimpses into my psyche". These first three books, which ARTNIK is publishing, open the door on his psyche and reveal a man who is much bigger and far more fascinating than his image.

My overwhelming impression of Strictly Private to Public Exposure was the honesty of the narrative. We are often urged to read autobiographies because they are open, frank, candid... yet they can be all that and still self-serving. Most people are cowards when it comes to exposing in print how they know themselves. Alexander is true to himself, which is a rare quality in a man never mind an autobiography. Whatever exception may be taken to Alexander's lifestyle and the causes he holds dear, I defy anyone who reads his memoirs not to enjoy them and end up admiring the person they reveal.

Nigel Dempster
*September 2002*

# Prologue

## THE MARQUESS OF BATH

My purpose is to reveal myself here on paper, at considerable length until, to the best of my ability, something approaching the entire Me has been laid open to view. The material comes from my journals, which I never show to anybody.

Their writing has been a central discipline within my life, involving a sustained stint which I set myself while I was still very young, always with a view to producing an autobiography before I died.

On the first page of each notebook is always inscribed the phrase *Strictly Private*. But it is now time for much of this material to be translated into a literary form intended for exposure to the world.

There are seven different categories into which this material falls:

❀ ancestry, parents and upbringing

❀ siblings and relatives

❀ power, authority and hierarchy

❀ career and activities

❀ love, sex and marital group

❀ fatherhood, children and futurity

❋ identity, worship and the Deity.

Using these categories as part of my chapter-headings I shall be switching between them as the whim takes me, and as irreverently as I might please, always hoping to entertain my reader, as much as to explain and to define myself.

Alexander Thynn
*Marquess of Bath*

# PART ONE

# FAMILY
# BACKGROUND

# Chapter 1

## Worship: The holy temple

By way of introduction I had best summarise the accounts that already exist of the curious background into which I was born and that I have made some use of, including essential information derived from the book on my family by David Burnett, and from my mother's own autobiography.

These sources have been combined with some original observations which would no doubt be disputed elsewhere.

I regard this as a necessary prelude, incidentally, because there is no way of comprehending the anxieties which fashioned me without perceiving them in the context of Longleat House and its traditions. Whether in acting to conform with those traditions, or in revolt against them, I am still the product of Longleat. For better or for worse, it has always been (and always will be) my life's stage.

So how should I write an appreciation of Longleat?

This vast Elizabethan stately home is the only stage that I have ever known, but it is also a magnificent one to find there beneath my feet. There is a mystique and legend about the place, such as might inspire embroidery and exaggeration of any kind. Take a glimpse at the way it is viewed nowadays by some people – notably the Ufologists. Their legend about the place runs something like this.

Longleat has always been a holy site. They would say that central Wessex abounds with such sites, and that Glastonbury, Stonehenge and Avebury are prominent examples. Yet strategically at the centre of this triangle stands Longleat, on land (as they argue) which may have been the holiest site of them all. They speculate that long before the priory which once occupied the site, it was an even holier place. They point to the saucer-shaped cradle of the park (an area just short of 1,000 acres/405 hectares) and proclaim sagely that this is the point where the first immigrants from outer space landed and garaged their vehicle, now discreetly buried beneath several fathoms of earth.

Permission has been requested for archaeological digs that would uncover the ship which transported them hither – but we have always managed to discourage such enthusiasm, asserting that their spades and bulldozers might derange some of the park's superb natural beauty. An idea which has never been disproved, however, gathers force, and it does furnish comfort for my family in that, if it turns out to be true, then when the day of the final holocaust approaches, the galactic ship will finally take flight, bearing the selected inhabitants of Earth (as if in some latter-day Noah's Ark) to a safer galaxy.

From my very persistence in residing there, I might assume that I am numbered amongst those chosen few.

In any case, the incentive exists, as you must well understand, for me to remain close to Longleat whenever life begins to look dangerous – although I dread the day when the Exodus panic really takes hold, and there is a sustained determination within a whole cult to come and dwell in what we do still regard as our home park.

But whether their speculation be true or false as a description of the way in which our known world will finally come to an end, this family temple does furnish for me at least an irrational status of serenity and security, such as they proclaim.

# Chapter 2

## Ancestry: The general picture

### The Sixteenth and Seventeenth Centuries

## SIR JOHN THYNN (1515–1580)

My family's involvement upon this scene dates back to 1540, when John Thynn was a mere twenty-five years old. He was my direct ancestor, of precisely thirteen generations back, and he then acquired the site upon which Longleat now stands – for the sum of £53.

This site contained the ruins of an ancient priory of the same name, which had formerly belonged to the Black Canons of St Augustine. They had fallen into disgrace relatively early in the trend towards dissolution, having a reputation for depravity which included rumours about the practice of witchcraft. Their goose was finally cooked when they started flaunting silver greyhounds embroidered upon their black habits. Their superiors, who had been tolerant of all previous misdemeanours, now decided to remove them from the priory, and it was eventually razed to the ground. The site upon which it had been standing was then acquired by a certain Sir John Horsey who sold it, later, to the young John Thynn.

All of John Thynn's ambition, spirit and life-long drive went into the rebuilding of Longleat – as a family seat this time, rather than as a building dedicated to any manner of religion. It had probably been his intention from the very start to use the site he had purchased to this end, which was in effect the creation of a launching-pad for his own family dynasty. But the construction work was only really commenced in 1568, when he was already in his fifties. So a little more explanation is needed about how the man had managed to emerge within Tudor society in a sufficient state of acquired wealth and affluence to be able to realise such an ambition.

John Thynn was a typical specimen of the new Protestant breed of rapaciously acquisitive, ruthlessly determined, shrewdly self-interested men on the make within the Tudor court. He was both truculent and difficult to please – a hard task-master, if not a slave-driver, obsessed with the desire to obtain the maximum return on any penny spent. *I have good reason* was the motto that he eventually chose for himself, but it might have been more in character of the man if the clause had been *I demand value for my money.*

John was the son of a Shropshire farmer. But it was under his uncle, William Thynn, who was the Chief Clerk to the Royal Kitchens, that he made his first entry upon court circles, soon thereafter to receive the patronage of the young Earl of Hertford, who was Jane Seymour's brother and Henry VIII's brother-in-law. And as his patron's political power increased, so too did John Thynn's own influence and affluence, no doubt in part from the profitable task of selling and dispersing the lands confiscated from the monasteries. The site of the 'Longlete' priory was indeed acquired during this period, even if at second hand.

After the death of Henry VIII, Hertford was initially the power behind the throne to Edward VI, and was created Duke of Somerset and Protector of the Realm, virtually ruling the country as guardian to the boy-king who was his nephew. In the company of his patron, John Thynn's own star was in the ascendant. In addition to all the methods for accumulating wealth (legal or otherwise) which came his way as a result of the posts he held, he was also acquiring invaluable experience in the building of Somerset House for his patron, stimulating personal ambitions which were later to be fulfilled.

Then in 1547, on the battlefield at Pinkie, he was knighted for valour against the Scots, or perhaps more deservedly as a measure of his prolonged services to the Protector, Somerset, who was riding at the head of the English army. Sir John's enemies later were to cast aspersions against the idea that he had been at all valiant on the battlefield, suggesting instead that he had spent the hours of combat cowering in a wagon. But in those days there were inadequate laws against libel and slander to deter such abuse from people who were, in all probability, intent on settling their own grievances against a man's reputation, which had somehow impinged upon their own advancement.

So now came the whole question of how Sir John could find acceptance within the Tudor court as a genuine nobleman, instead of being permanently disesteemed as the common upstart that indeed he was. Little was authoritatively known about his true ancestry, other than that his immediate forebears came from Shropshire, and included lawyers as well as farmers as their kin. But he required more detail than that if he was to receive the acceptance of society, while contending with all the prejudices and the snobberies of court circles in that day and age.

What he really needed was a long Norman ancestry to replace the suspicion of Saxon heritage, which was then regarded as plebeian. And by this time he had doubtless all the power and influence that might be required to cook the records so that he might appear to have the authentic credentials for such lineage, when they were in fact absent. By my own conjecture, the subsequent story might well run like this.

The genealogists of the day had probably discovered that a few generations back the Thynns had married into a genuinely Norman family, the Botevilles, or Botfields as the name was sometimes styled, with descent from Sir Geoffrey de Boteville, who had come over to England from Poitiers to assist King John in his power struggle with his barons. Both Thynns and Botfields were by the approach of Tudor times living in Shropshire, and the genealogists made it their business to present the Thynns as the patrilineal descendants of the de Botevilles.

I say this in the belief that the true origin of the Thynn family name is the Saxon adjective meaning what it might obviously appear to. All other descriptions exist – like Bigge, Tall, Little, Small, Short, Slim, Fatt, Broad or Narrow. So there would have been something astonishingly remiss in the reproductive abilities of 'thin' Saxons if they never left any trace of their visual appearance within common English surnames. But to furnish Sir John with Norman ancestry, it was necessary for them to play around with the name Thynn so that it might sound to have different origins.

In the vagueness which existed in those days concerning precise family origins, there was probably no difficulty in passing off a previous direct ancestor by the name of John Thynn as being a Boteville, from the family who had married into the Thynns. All they had to say was that this John Boteville was in the habit of describing himself as being 'of the inne', which later became Thynne by elision – the whole purpose (it was said) being to avoid confusion with another John Boteville currently living in those parts, with the final 'e' (of Thynne) now appended to the name, more often than not, to match the contemporary spelling of the word 'inne'. No one has satisfactorily established whether the relevant inn was supposed to have been a large dwelling-place, a public house, or an inn of court, but it was more probably the latter because law had been one of the family's principal concerns. And by the end of these machinations, Sir John emerged with the genealogical status and social regard that were so necessary for the fulfilment of his ambition.

One immediate result of his newly recognised nobility was that he became more eligible as a bachelor within the eyes of the lesser nobility, so that Sir John was now able to find himself a worthy wife. This was Christian Gresham, the twenty-four-year-old daughter of Sir Richard Gresham, London's Lord Mayor and one of London's wealthiest new rich. She was to bear him eleven children, although only five survived to become adults. But she also brought him additional wealth and land, and she stood by him in loyal support during the lean years which were to follow.

Sir John's misfortune was that the Duke of Somerset was worsted as a result of a power struggle with the Earl of Warwick (or the Duke of Northumberland as he was soon created.) In his capacity as Somerset's steward, Sir John was aware how both the duke and he might expect similar treatment, and both of them were indeed carted off to the Tower on successive occasions, in 1549 and in 1551. The charges of treasonable activity didn't stick, so they were initially released. But the new ruling clique was determined at the very least to strip them of all political influence. And on a second attempt they made out a better case against Somerset, who was promptly beheaded, and they almost got Sir John on the charge of embezzlement, although he was ultimately saved by his marital association with the Gresham family. Nonetheless, he was obliged to pay substantial fines, even though the charges remained unproven. What probably stuck even more in his gullet than the obligation to part with some of his dubiously acquired wealth was the requirement to write humble letters to Northumberland, pleading that he was really an honest man.

His fortunes took a turn for the better when Mary acceded to the throne, for his arch-enemy Northumberland was himself executed after attempting to take the Crown on behalf of his niece, Lady Jane Grey. Sir John was then released from the Tower. Yet despite his all too evident disaffiliation from the previous ruling clique, as a Protestant there could still be no real place for him within Queen Mary's entourage. His competence as an administrator, however, had never been in doubt, and his experience of life in the Tower befitted him especially for appointment as the Comptroller of the young Princess Elizabeth's household, in that her own freedom was currently under her sister's restraint.

It was a role that Sir John may well have regarded with unease, knowing as he did how servants (if powerful enough) were often called upon to follow their employers to the scaffold. So while being none too arduously attendant upon the young Princess's welfare, he managed to keep his nose clean, thus surviving into Elizabeth's accession to the throne, and even retaining for a while his post as the Comptroller to her household.

Sir John may have been an uncouth, domineering, formidable rogue of ill-gotten wealth, shrewdly cunning and essentially ruthless, but he was now emerging as an eminent Elizabethan, with a far healthier climate for the development of his own interests. Even though the post of Comptroller was soon awarded to another, particular services were still demanded of him by the young Queen. He was also the Member of Parliament for Wiltshire. Yet by and large he had learned his lesson, in that he had now become a far more cautious and politically less ambitious man, content to focus the remainder of his days upon the greatest of all his ambitions – which was to build the new Longleat.

In one way or another he had been squaring up to this task ever since he acquired the site in 1540, preparing the land and generally renovating the ruins of the old priory so that it became a large habitable dwelling once again. But in 1567 there was a great fire, from causes unknown. (Sir John had accumulated enemies, as well as wealth, by his truculence towards neighbours, which included petty warfare against those whom he regarded as poaching scoundrels.) But this destruction by fire of all that he cherished most, which would have shattered some lesser man, in fact turned out to furnish him with the opportunity of a lifetime. For it was a year later, in 1568, with a good twenty-five years of experience in building to his cred-it, that he was at liberty to start afresh upon the construction of his archi-tectural dream palace.

It should be noted how this was a fabulously ostentatious task, and one that hitherto could not have been undertaken, if only for the reason of attracting too much attention to his dubiously acquired riches. But it was also a daring enterprise in that it set out to build something in a style that had never yet been ventured upon British soil – a real harbinger of the Renaissance, in effect, in that its architectural innovations had taken this long to creep northwards through Europe and reach England.

Smithson may have been the master mason, or perhaps even its architect, but it was Sir John himself who demanded the inspiration and provided the compulsive drive and the tenacity of purpose for its comple-tion. Whoever worked on the place was carefully enacting what their employer had planned, and they were essentially introducing the new concept of an ornate Italianate style a rich façade flaunting a myriad windows, false pillars, rondelles containing busts, and a roof surmounted with false battlements (since replaced by a balustrade), and with an eccentric array of chimneys and domes breaking up the severe outline of the rectangular silhouette.

So in this manner Longleat House, more or less as I know it today, arose like a phoenix from the ashes of the renovated Longlete Priory. And some might say that this was the finest example of High Elizabethan architecture within the stately homes of Britain. It rose to dominate the peaceful landscape within its cradling park – the ambition of one ruthless old rogue fulfilled (or nearly so) within the latter days of his life.

Christian Gresham, Sir John's first wife, had not lived to witness the building of Longleat, for she had died in 1565. Yet within a year Sir John had acquired another Lord Mayor's daughter to be his bride: one Dorothy Wroughton. And he fathered on her a second strand of the Thynne family – some eight children in all, seven of which were sons. If all of the male issue from the first brood were now to perish, he would still be left with descendant heirs to Longleat.

Sir John's final mark upon the English political scene was in his lavish entertainment of Queen Elizabeth on the occasion of her Royal Progress through the West Country. She had stated that it was her royal pleasure to cast her countenance upon this new palace that he was building. But lavish hospitality was entirely out of character for Sir John, and he did his utmost to escape from such an onerous duty, making all manner of excuses to put off the costly day of her descent upon his scene.

To start with it may have been all right to plead that the new house was still insufficiently complete to house her in regal style, but after 1572 it became common knowledge that he himself, and his entire family, had already taken up residence in the building, so it clearly couldn't be that uncomfortable. And when he claimed even now that it wouldn't be safe for her to visit, since there was a disease within the household, she finally lost her temper and declared him to be a scoundrel. Whereupon Sir John promptly made amends, and did his utmost to make the visit a huge success – as indeed it was finally proclaimed to be by no lesser person than the Queen herself.

Sir John lived on at Longleat until 1580. He died after a short illness when he was sixty-five, which was then regarded as being quite a ripe old age.

**Found**er of a **dyn**asty and **build**er of a **state**ly **home**,

with **mom**entary **glimps**es of as**signed nat**ional **pow**er,
you en**dowed** a **long line** of **success**ive **Thynns**
with **lin**eage a**war**eness. We sa**lute** your **vis**ionary in**tent**.
Re**lent**less in **ruth**less pur**suit** of **pers**onal **goals**,
you **bold**ly pro**mot**ed an e**goc**entric i**deal**,
**keel-haul**ing your **many** (re**pri**sal-**bent**)
en**emies** be**neath** the **hulk** of your **prince**ly **mon**ument.
**Pon**dering **naught oth**er than the '**good reas**on'
of **seas**onable **self-int**erest, you **trod** the **plodd**ed
**road** of **wish**ful am**bit**ion, de**void** of **glo**ry,
but a **stor**y **full** of **pri**vately en**trench**ed en**rich**ment.
  The jutting chin and scowling glare pronounce
  determined resolution with a bounce.

## SIR JOHN THYNN II (1555–1604)

Sir John left behind him a feuding family. Dorothy, his second wife, resisted the inheritance of the estate by John, his first wife's eldest son. She remained in residence for some months, parading of an evening with her entire household up on the roof at Longleat, while the legitimate heir negotiated her eventual departure to a house in neighbouring Corsley – the house, in fact, which had housed the family just after the fire of 1567. Even at this small distance, however, the relationship between the two branches of the family festered until Dorothy remarried to Sir Walter Raleigh's brother Carew, going to live with him on his own estate, and thus centring her own brood upon a different homestead.

  John (junior) wasn't a patch on his father, but it should be stated that he had lived a difficult life. He was only ten at the death of his mother Christian, and was thereafter disliked by his stepmother and overshadowed by his father. He almost was disinherited altogether by his father because of his seduction of one Lucy Mervyn, who claimed that he had fathered her eldest son. But Sir John regarded her as unsuitable to become Longleat's chatelaine. John (junior) bowed to his father's wishes, ditched the luckless Lucy (who was later to wed Lord Audley) and himself followed what was fast becoming a family tradition by marrying Joan, the daughter of another Lord Mayor of London, Sir Roland Hayward.

The marriage may have reconciled father and son, but Joan never proved any better fitted to the running of Longleat than her ill-esteemed husband managed to be. By emulating the domineering tactics without the shrewd cunning to set them to useful purpose, John inspired as much dislike and resentment locally as ever his father had done. And in the judgement of posterity he must be criticised for letting slip the essential opportunity to complete the building of Longleat from his father's plans and with the assembled team of masons. The completion was finally achieved more gradually, over the course of several centuries, in accordance with varying intentions and designs.

His own real interests were split between the hunting of game and the social life of London society. As far as public service was concerned, he so displeased the Queen's Privy Council, which accused him of both fraud and mismanagement, that he was ultimately fined and dismissed from his Stewardship of the Royal Manors. Nevertheless, like his father, he acquired the distinction of a knighthood, for no better reason than that (Scottish) King James, on his accession to the British throne in 1603, required support from the principal English landowners.

The next big drama within the family was when his son, Thomas, declared his intention to marry Lord Audley's daughter, whose mother was the former Lucy Mervyn, his father's rejected love. This didn't go down at all well, opening up an additional possibility for disinheritance. But Lucy Audley eventually managed to prevail upon the father, by unrecorded methods, to withdraw his objections to this legitimate, if belated, blending of their family genes.

The marriage was proclaimed, and they had issue. Nor did father and son have sufficient time to become irreconciled again, for soon after the marriage had been consummated, Sir John II learned of a plot to kidnap him, and fled to London where concealment could more easily be arranged – quite apart from the fact that life in the capital could be appreciated more lavishly.

He only returned to Longleat in time to fall ill and die, to be buried alongside Sir John I in the family vault at Longbridge Deverill. His wife Joan set up house on their estate in Shropshire, becoming patron to the composer John Maynard – by whom a book of his lute music was dedicated to her – while Longleat itself passed into the ownership of his son Thomas.

It should be noted incidentally that in the spelling of the family name, Thynn was preferred to Thynne by both father and son. It was only in subsequent generations that the final 'e' was always included, in line with the first Sir John's machinations to acquire Norman ancestry.

## SIR THOMAS THYNN (1574-1640)

Thomas was clearly a man of far greater calibre than his father had been. Soon after he had inherited Longleat, he was knighted and appointed Ambassador to the Netherlands, then subsequently made High Sheriff of three separate counties, as well as Member of Parliament for Wiltshire. But he managed to avoid any too open alignment with either King or Parliament during the period of polarisation after Charles I ascended to the throne. From the little that has been left on record concerning his life and career, it is a matter for personal regret that we do not know more about him, for he is a direct ancestor, of whom I might have some good cause to feel proud.

What is known is that Sir Thomas was loved and revered by each of his successive wives, Maria Audley being followed by Catherine Howard, a niece of the Duke of Norfolk. Our marital relationship with the latter family means, incidentally, that her own Thynn progeny might also claim to be of royal descent – a line which carries through to myself.

## SIR JAMES THYNNE (1605-1670)
## SIR HENRY FREDERICK THYNNE (1615–1681)

Between the two broods of children fathered by Sir Thomas there was to arise much acrimony and litigation – all because the second wife, Catherine, persuaded him when delirious on his deathbed, to rewrite his will so that her own brood received a far higher proportion of the wealth and properties than any from Maria's brood.

And the quarrelling was to endure for an entire generation, Sir James (Maria's eldest surviving son) winning the opening skirmish by having Catherine and her son, Sir Henry Frederick Thynne, thrown out of Longleat with all their belongings. After initiating such chaos Catherine was soon to die, but the two half-brothers were to battle for many a year to come.

In his youth, James had travelled and had seen active service in the Netherlands at the outset of what had been intended as a military career. He married the beautiful Lady Isabella Holland, daughter of the Earl of Holland, and was knighted on joining Charles I's court. But Henry Frederick in the other corner – whose first names derived from his godfather, the King of Denmark – was also knighted by Charles I after marrying Mary, the daughter of Lord Coventry, and he was now settled on his estate up in Gloucestershire. When it came to the Civil War, however, Sir Henry Frederick came out in much more open support of the Royalist cause, was thereupon stripped of his lands by Parliament, and was therefore in a far better position to gain royal favour, and promotion, at the time of the Restoration. He was then raised to the very brink of nobility, when he was created a baronet, going by the name of Sir Henry Frederick Thynne of Warminster.

Not that any real blame can be attributed to Sir James for neglecting to fulfil his military promise by rallying to the King's standard at the outbreak of hostilities. Examples of what happened to the property of those who resisted the will of the Parliamentary forces were easy enough to observe on the very doorstep of Longleat, where Woodhouse Castle was razed to the ground and Nunney Castle left nothing but a shell. There may have been words of reproach from the Royalist camp that Sir James had been unwilling to risk his neck for the King, yet by his caution he almost certainly saved Longleat from destruction. Nor was he by any means disgraced at the time of the Restoration, if we judge from the fact that he was then appointed High Sheriff of Wiltshire.

His wife Lady Isabella had enjoyed the Civil War rather more festively than he himself did. The marriage had in fact failed relatively early, but she then proceeded to acquire for herself a reputation of being one of the most libertine of courtesans attending the King's court at Oxford. She is described as dancing on the banks of the Thames holding a lute and clad only in loose and very inadequate attire. By the time of the Restoration she had deserted her husband completely and moved to London, where she involved herself in numerous affairs, giving birth to various love-children who were to turn up, subsequently, with monotonous regularity, to put in their claims to the Longleat inheritance after Sir James had died childless.

## THOMAS THYNNE (1648–1682)

Litigation between the half-brothers had continued right up to the time of Sir James' death, with the occasional half-hearted attempt at reconciliation in compromise, which invariably broke down in further insult or outrage. Nor was the battle concluded with his death, since he had bequeathed everything to his nephew Tom (o' Ten Thousand) Thynne, who was the son of his full brother Thomas, himself recently deceased. And with Tom came the opportunity for Sir John Thynne's dynasty to attain its long-desired goal of ennoblement – not for actually doing something great, yet by way of compensation to the family for his assassination.

I shall offer two different versions as to how this came about.

Tom o' Ten Thousand inherited Longleat in 1670 when in his thirties, and in some ways he epitomised the Restoration rake as a wealthy wom-aniser of somewhat foppish appearance. (The 'Ten Thousand', incidental-ly, indicated his estimated annual income from the Longleat estates, which in the currency of those days was regarded as excessive.) Amongst his clos-est friends was the Duke of Monmouth, Charles II's illegitimate son, with whom he frequented London's brothels and gaming-houses.

Tom also had political ambitions. He was the Member of Parliament for Wiltshire and, more dangerously, the Colonel of the Regiment of Horse in the Wiltshire Militia. By 1680, however, Charles II was beginning to have cause for suspicion about the political intentions of both Monmouth and Tom Thynne. They were jointly cultivating the Exclusionist cause throughout the West Country. This was a movement which sought to exclude all Roman Catholics from the throne, and was calculated to per-mit Monmouth to inherit the Crown, in preference to Charles' younger brother James. And this worried Charles, who firmly believed it to be in the best interests of the country he governed to abide by the constitution-al expectations for succession, rather than to risk a second Civil War after all the ravages of the first. He therefore removed the Regiment of Horse from Tom's command and attempted, inadequately, to dissuade

Monmouth from his treasonous ambitions.

It was at this point that Tom married Lady Elizabeth Percy, a mere fifteen-year-old, but already the widow of the Earl of Ogle. This first marriage had been sufficient to render her rich, but even more significantly, she was the sole heir to the Duke of Northumberland who had recently died, leaving her with the expectation of inheriting a vast estate up north. In the meantime her grandmother, the Dowager Duchess, was concerned to get her spliced to the right person, even before there could be any realistic talk about consummating the marriage. First it was to Lord Ogle; and then, after he died, to Tom Thynne.

So the official version of Tom Thynne's assassination runs like this.

Elizabeth the child-bride was in Holland, having quarrelled with her grandmother. There she met the glamorous Count Konigsmark, a notorious Swedish rake, and fell madly in love for the first time. And Konigsmark, regarding Tom Thynne as the sole obstacle between himself and a substantial fortune, came over secretly to London, in the company of three villainous henchmen, to rid himself of his rival. Attempts to challenge Tom to a duel came to nothing, so a plan was evolved to gun him down by blunderbuss as he rode in his carriage. This was finally staged in no less a street than Pall Mall, not far from the royal residence of         St James' Palace.

There was public shock and general consternation as to how such a thing could happen in broad daylight on the streets of London – also bewilderment as to why anyone should wish to murder someone so gregariously popular as Tom. All manner of theories were whispered abroad. But evidence quickly emerged that Konigsmark was in town, and a scandalous relationship was rumoured between him and Tom's child-bride. In the hue and cry which followed, the authorities soon rounded up all four suspects and put them on trial. The three henchmen were convicted and hanged in Pall Mall, at the scene of their crime, but Konigsmark was curiously acquitted and permitted to leave the country. He never did win the hand in marriage of Lady Elizabeth. He was to die a few years later, as a soldier of fortune, while taking part in the siege of Argos against the Turks.

So much for the official version, but I shall now venture some fresh ideas.

In 1682, the year of the assassination, Tom Thynne was regarded by Charles II as being politically dangerous – the one person who might be capable of rallying the West Country to Monmouth's banner in the event of a rebellion. So the simplest and surest method of thwarting his favourite son's undesirable ambitions was for the King to devise a plan for Tom to be assassinated. And to this end his agents in Holland may have suggested to Konigsmark that he could win the hand of the lady he desired, and even get away with murder, if he took it into his head to dispose of Tom Thynne. Whether or not Charles' agents were required to assist any further in Konigsmark's designs remains dubious, even if the site chosen for the murder was suspiciously close to the King's own doorstep.

It was safe to assume that the English public would be well pleased by the conviction of the four undesirable aliens accused of the crime. Yet Konigsmark himself kept well behind the scenes during the actual perpetration of the deed. Even so, it is astonishing that he was actually acquitted. It was clear to John Evelyn (in his diary of that time) that the jury who tried the case had been corrupted with bribes, and some of the judge's rulings were outrageous even by contemporary standards. He went further than merely advising them to acquit Konigsmark – whose own bearing, from the moment of his arrest, was as if he expected that this would be the outcome, almost as if he had been promised an acquittal if ever the need should arise – provided that he never revealed the source of his patronage, which in reality may have been from no less a person than the King himself.

What is perhaps even more surprising is the way Charles II hastened to bestow honours upon the Thynne family, arranging for Tom's corpse to be interred at Westminster Abbey. And since the Longleat inheritance was now passing over to Sir Henry Frederick's branch of the family – to his son Sir Thomas, in fact, who had now become the second baronet – feelings about a miscarriage of justice organised by the Crown were perhaps minimised by the hastily expedient elevation of Sir Thomas to the peerage – which happened within a couple of months of the cousin's assassination. He was to be known thenceforward as the 1st Viscount Weymouth.

No one from his side of the long-standing fraternal divide had any further cause for complaint.

And nor have I, if it comes to that. Without of course condoning any of the criminal decisions that may have been taken along the course of this history, as a descendant of Sir Henry Frederick, rather than of Sir James, I acknowledge that it does stand to my advantage that matters were resolved in this way.

# Chapter 3

## Ancestry: The general picture

The later Seventeenth to mid-Eighteenth Centuries

### THOMAS THYNNE,
### THE 1ST VISCOUNT WEYMOUTH (1640-1714)

Sir Henry Frederick's brood of children were a closely-knit bunch who remained in concerned relationship with one another throughout their lives. They were also ambitious and efficient. The eldest brother (now created Viscount Weymouth) was firmly at the head of the family, supported by their respect and affection. Even prior to his inheritance of Longleat, the young Thomas had acquired some distinction: to start with as a critic and antiquarian at Oxford University, then as the Member of Parliament for Oxford, in addition to being Lord Lieutenant of Wiltshire, and then appointed Special Envoy for Charles II to the Swedish Court. This latter honour was during the time he belonged to the Duke of York's household just after the Restoration, (long prior to his accession to the throne as James II) while Thomas was only twenty-six years old.

By 1672 Thomas was also a married man, with both sons and daughters: his wife was Frances Finch, daughter of the Earl of Winchelsea. She was a good lady, of nervous disposition, who had brought a large estate of 22,000 acres/8,900 hectares into the family as part of her dowry. This was at Carrickmacross in County Monaghan, immediately south of what is now the North Ireland border. Of his two surviving brothers, James was a jovial womanising bachelor, and Henry Frederick (through whose line the family was eventually to trace its patrilineal descent) was a staid but competent model of respectability – a successful civil servant who in turn was Keeper of the Royal Library, Secretary to the Chancellor, Clerk to the Privy Council, and Treasurer to Charles II's widow.

It may be of interest to point out that through Frances Finch the Thynne family's kinship with the royal family was enhanced (for the first time since Sir Thomas Thynne had married Catherine Lyte-Howard) in that she herself bore indirect descent from Henry VII through his daughter Mary Tudor (the sister of Henry VIII), who was married initially to King Louis XII of France, but then after being widowed, to Charles Brandon, Duke of Suffolk. They had a daughter, Lady Frances Brandon, who somewhat confusingly married Henry Grey, a different Duke of Suffolk (formerly Marquess of Dorset), who was the father of Lady Jane Grey – both of them being executed after his attempt to place her on the throne in place of of Princess Mary. But there was a younger sister, Lady Katherine Grey, who married Edward Seymour, Earl of Hertford, whose great-granddaughter Lady Mary Seymour married the Earl of Winchelsea – and their daughter was the Lady Frances Finch who married the 1st Viscount Weymouth.

Returning to the year 1682, however, just after Tom o' Ten Thousand had been assassinated and Sir Thomas had been created the 1st Viscount Weymouth, the major issue concerning the family was whether Tom's child-bride Lady Elizabeth might not insist that Longleat House should be regarded officially as her own place of residence. She had never had the opportunity to move in, but the situation was delicate in that there were some who whispered how she herself could have been implicated in Tom's murder. It turned out, in fact, to be the young girl's wish to get the whole Thynne saga firmly behind her, which she achieved by wedding the Duke of Somerset. This was a sufficiently significant step up the social ladder for her to cede, with grace, to the Thynne family's insistence that Longleat House belonged to themselves.

There was still the Monmouth rebellion for them to contend with. It finally erupted in 1685, immediately after James II's accession to the throne. Thomas had already been obliged to endure a certain antagonism from those who worked on the Longleat estate, in that his own political affiliation was Loyalist rather than Exclusionist. And when Monmouth landed at Lyme Regis in Dorset to rally the West Country to his banner, there were quite a few who joined the rebel ranks, principal among whom was Captain Kidd, who had been the head gamekeeper at Longleat in Tom o' Ten Thousand's day. He was to become the only man knighted on the field of battle by Monmouth.

As the rebel forces approached Longleat, there was considerable trepidation concerning what their attitude towards the new occupants might be. Thomas found it wiser to remain up in London, while Frances quickly journeyed to visit friends in Salisbury. Monmouth fought an indecisive skirmish at Norton St Philip, on his withdrawal from Bath. He then occupied Frome, and the local militia in Warminster deserted to his cause. Rebel scouts even visited Longleat for purposes which remain uncertain. But Monmouth and his rabble (which they claimed to muster 30,000 men) then marched suddenly to Sedgemoor, which at that time was an outlying part of the Longleat estate – and it was here that they were finally routed by the Loyalist forces, amongst whose commanders was the Duke of Somerset who had so recently married Tom o' Ten Thousand's young widow.

The fleeing rebels were quickly rounded up and dispatched, without mercy, after Judge Jeffreys' bloody assize. It took five strokes of the axe to get Monmouth properly decapitated, up in London, after being found disguised as a woman and hiding in a ditch on the outskirts of the New Forest. The wretched Captain Kidd fared even worse, getting hanged, drawn and quartered on the beach at Lyme Regis – which is probably the fate that would have been dished out to Tom Thynne if he had survived the assassination attempt, for he would almost certainly have thrown in his lot with Monmouth. Instead of that, he was left peacefully at rest in Westminster Abbey, amongst the country's most revered and loyal citizens.

The Monmouth rebellion, which was the last occasion for any armed battle upon English soil, may have been little more than a disturbing hiccough within the life of the 1st Viscount. He had in fact already embarked upon his programme of good works at Longleat, to modernise the building and to set the estate in efficient working order; and it was to this programme that he now returned. Previous generations had lapsed in their care of the place, particularly at fault being Tom o' Ten Thousand, who had been more of a London man. But when Thomas and Frances took up their residence, they displayed an abundance of good intentions, their concern being to create a little paradise, on a basis of mutual service and benefit between landlord and community.

And a considerable success Thomas made of it, whether in terms of the estate's annual revenue, which soon reached £12,000, or the total acreage which reached 50,000 (20,235 hectares) in his lifetime. Most of all, perhaps, his success may be measured in terms of the goodwill of his tenants.

His modernisation of the house interior was not to enduring effect. For example, there was a chapel introduced within the West Wing, which has now given way to a billiards room and service flat. But there were some alterations which were indeed to last. The roof sprouted a balustrade (instead of battlements) which he surmounted with a series of stone statues depicting an aristocracy of immortals to watch over the Thynne family dynasty – figures carefully chosen by himself, including Alexander the Great, Henry V and Boadicea. The front door of the house was also aggrandised, and a special livery in mustard and black was designed for those who stood in attendance upon the family (although gold and black were more officially the family colours.)

What changed most of all, however, were the general surroundings to the house, for Thomas was impassioned by the idea of gardens, and inspired in particular by Versailles. He employed George London to lay out a vast complex of ornate terraced flowerbeds, with symmetrical paths and avenues, to furnish Longleat with a decorative environment which stretched for the most part eastwards, across the leat (having diverted 'the long lete' with a canal), and on up into what is now the safari park. And the whole family, when gathered, took much delight in the home-grown fruit to be harvested at Longleat.

Blessed though they were with good fortune in so many ways, Thomas and Frances were out of luck when it came to raising a family. Smallpox was the great killer disease in those days, and miscarriages blighted other hopes for offspring. But for a long while they did have a son and heir, in the person of Henry. Sickly at the start, and then too fat, he dismayed his tutors who were unable to tailor him into the material that his father desired. On the other hand, Thomas was in no hurry to get him married off and thus settled – particularly when it was the Earl of Pembroke, from the neighbouring stately home of Wilton House, who was seeking an appropriate match for his thirteen-year-old daughter. (He disapproved of the Pembrokes, the Earl as a drunken brawler, and the Countess as a tart.) Thomas told him politely at the start, but then on repetition, more bluntly, why he felt disinclined to encourage such a financially beneficial marital alliance between the two most powerful Wiltshire families. And the relationship between the two noblemen was thenceforward soured.

A close friend from the 1st Viscount's days at Oxford had been Thomas Ken, who was later to become the Bishop of Bath and Wells. How he ever rose that high within the clerical hierarchy came as a surprise to many since, as a canon at Winchester, he had refused permission for Nell Gwynne to be lodged in his house when accompanying Charles II (as his mistress) upon some official business in the town. Yet it was Charles himself who promoted Ken, against the ambitions of others, having been impressed by the man's devout sincerity.

This was not the end of all trouble for the new Bishop, however. With six others he received a spell of imprisonment under James II for forbidding his Declaration of Indulgence to be read out from the diocesan pulpits. Yet with the advent of William and Mary to the throne after the Bloodless Revolution of 1688, he refused to transfer his oath of allegiance from James, on the grounds that once given, it could not be forsworn. In the company of all such non-jurors, he was deprived of his see.

So at this juncture in his life, the Bishop turned to his aristocratic friend from university days, which led to his taking up residence on the top floor at Longleat for a period of some twenty years. And during this time he exerted a profound influence upon the 1st Viscount, becoming what some might describe as his conscience.

Thomas thus acquired a reputation for good deeds,which he himself regarded as spontaneous enough but which the friends of his youth were inclined to regard as having been inspired by his devout friend, the Bishop. And as an example of such benevolence, somewhere between the two of them, they founded the Lord Weymouth School at Warminster.

Notable too is the fact that a portion of the West Wing was now transformed into a chapel for the household's daily worship. Not that its interior ever matched the architectural finery of equivalent chapels in other stately homes, but it was in any case evidence of the devout spirit which prevailed at Longleat over that particular historical period.

The influence of Bishop Ken was not wholly spiritual. It should also be noted that he contributed materially to Longleat in bequeathing his fine library of books to it. The 1st Viscount himself had a fine library. So when all this was added to the thirty odd books of exceptional value that had previously been collected by the first Sir John, the house could be said to have embarked upon a tradition, which subsequent generations have felt obliged to sustain by making their own manner of contribution to the collection. And mention too must be made of the portrait paintings by Kneller and Lely, commissioned by Thomas, in addition to Flemish tapestries, lacquered screens, silver flagons, rare clocks and inlaid writing tables, all brought into the house at this time.

Thomas' official career had continued to make steady progress, despite the fact that he never really quite made it into the history books. He was periodically in and out of royal favour, even on such a relatively minor issue as whether or not to continue as the Lord Lieutenant of Wiltshire. He was appointed first by Charles II, lost the post under James II, appointed again under William and Mary, only to lose it again under Anne.

He was always an active member of the House of Lords, and along with the Earl of Pembroke, whom he had so recently offended on the issue of marital ties, he was sent to Holland with an official letter inviting William of Orange to take over the government. What was galling, however, was the way William greeted Pembroke with affection, because he was a friend already, while choosing to ignore the wretched Thomas – and this episode was in part responsible for kindling his sympathy with the non-jurors, led by Bishop Ken.

So it was only under Queen Anne that his political career ripened, and despite the loss of the lord lieutenancy, he was appointed to the Privy Council, and created Secretary of Trade and the Plantations. In the latter capacity he was responsible for introducing the Lord Weymouth pine to Britain, which was useful for ship masts in that it grew tall and slender. But in truth this was a bit of a cheat, in that the name really derived from one George Weymouth, totally unrelated, who first discovered this pine growing in Maine. All Thomas did was to arrange for its importation, and prefix a Lord in front of the Weymouth in the tree's official appellation.

Thomas had his bouts of ill health. In fact in 1667, when he was laid low with the gout, he was never expected to recover – although he did. And in any case he managed to outlive all his male relatives, both his own and the succeeding generation, leaving him sadly without any grandsons from male issue. Family legend has it that he was twice offered an earldom during his final years. Yet without any male heir from his own loins, and with the inheritance of Longleat required by family entail to pass through the male line of descent from Sir John Thynne, he felt there was really not much point in accumulating any additional honours. He was more inclined to suppose that the whole line would soon be extinct, or too distant in blood ties for him to trouble himself.

In 1712 his wife Frances died, and within two years it would seem that his will to continue with life had been severely depleted. So he followed suit. He was then seventy-four years old.

## HENRY FREDERICK THYNNE JR (1671-1703)
## THOMAS THYNNE OF OLD WINDSOR
## (1687-1710)
## &
## THOMAS THYNNE, THE 2ND VISCOUNT
## WEYMOUTH (1710–1751)

Succession indeed there was through the line of his youngest brother, Henry Frederick, who married one Dorothy Phillips, producing yet another Thomas Thynne as their son, who was to become known as Thomas Thynne of Old Windsor. He was to die young, however, although not before the death of his cousin Henry, the 1st Viscount's own son. And it was as heir presumptive to the Longleat estate that he married the Lady Mary Villiers, daughter of the Earl of Jersey. He himself died shortly before the 1st Viscount, leaving his wife pregnant. And when the child turned out to be a boy, there was considerable excitement, in that great-grandfather Sir Henry Frederick's branch of the family once again had an heir.

So with a devotion to tradition that was beginning to become obsessive, the boy was yet again named Thomas, acquiring nobility at the tender age of four, and thus becoming known to the world as the 2nd Viscount Weymouth, the Crown having made special arrangements at the time of Tom o' Ten Thousand's assassination to ensure that  the title, then endowed, could pass down to any of Sir Henry Frederick's male descendants.

Let us consider the situation. Here was a four-year-old boy who had never known his father, being brought up by a vain and extravagant young woman who was even then only twenty-three years old. She knew next to nothing about the Thynne family traditions, and there were few to whom she could turn to learn about them. It was a situation which required a husband, of course, and this she rapidly found in the person of George, Lord Landsdown. Indolent and reckless, he was a dramatist and minor poet who wrote a number of unremarkable plays. Shortly after his marriage to Lady Mary, he was appointed Treasurer of the Royal Household, but his political career was curtailed when, in 1714 after the death of Queen Anne, he threw in his lot with James Stewart, the Old Pretender, and – perhaps inspired by Tom o' Ten Thousand's unrealised ambition incited a small uprising in the West Country, in reward for which he was imprisoned for three years in the Tower.

Yet the two of them had been appointed joint guardians to the young Thomas, who was then raised in the belief that Longleat would only become his property at their death – which was in fact false. Longleat was to become his automatically, as soon as he attained the age of twenty-one.

It cannot be said that Lord and Lady Landsdown were much concerned about the welfare of the young Thomas, an extremely ugly child whose upbringing was entrusted largely to a spinster nanny, whom he adored. (The initiation of a new family tradition perhaps?) After the stepfather's release from the Tower they all moved into Longleat, but it was a curious situation in that they all relied so much on the young Thomas' survival, without feeling emotionally involved in it. He was pampered with the luxury furnished by the estate, without either parental concern or guidance. The sickly unloved child was soon transformed into a spoiled brat, obstinately self-willed, and yet lacking any disciplined sense of purpose. So the rule of discipline was severely applied by a succession of tutors encouraged to emphasise that he was supposed to emerge as 'a young nobleman' (whatever that phrase might have been intended to imply).

By the time he had reached the age of twelve, however, Lord Landsdown had departed from Longleat because his marriage had failed. Lady Mary, who was weak-willed and coquettish, decided that something had gone awry with her son's development. So she switched tactics, now permitting total freedom from discipline, whereupon the boy grew unruly and his temper a lot worse. And with the knowledge at last that Longleat belonged to him only, he began contradicting her instructions, and thus undermining her authority with the servants. When the young Thomas wrote to the trustees in an attempt to dismiss his tutors, they decided contrarily that the only sensible solution was to send him to Eton, which blunted his arrogance in that he was then obliged to mingle with boys of a disposition similar to himself.

Another tactic thought up by his mother and the trustees to induce the young Thomas to become more humane was to marry him off at an early age. The bride they selected for him was Elizabeth Sackville, the fourteen-year-old daughter of the Earl of Dorset. Thomas himself was packed off on a prolonged European tour to complete his education – and to avoid the embarrassing possibility, no doubt, that he might insist on the marriage's consummation before his bride was emotionally prepared for such an event. The two children never did get round to it, though, for Elizabeth fell

ill and died while Thomas was still in France. Moreover, on finally returning to Longleat in 1731 aged twenty-one, he decided he'd had enough of
people arranging his life for him, and persuaded his mother to take up her
residence elsewhere (in Berkshire). They were never reconciled, and four
years later she died.

Of rather more enduring influence over the young man was Lord
Landsdown's niece, Mary Carteret (or Granville), who on marriage became
Mrs Delany. (Some of her portrait silhouettes which she cut from black
paper are preserved at Longleat up in the Old Library.) In the absence of
any stronger maternal influence, it was she who now undertook to guide
the attention of this vain yet physically unattractive young horror to some
inappropriately beautiful and sweet-tempered young filly – on the theory
that being mistress of Longleat would compensate for it all. And the girl
selected for this honour was a relative of hers, Louisa Carteret, daughter of
the Earl of Granville.

Louisa was in fact related to her future husband too, as his second
cousin once removed, through lines of descent that I should perhaps
explain – not least because it will show how the 1st Viscount's genes, and
the royal descent of his wife Frances Finch, were reintegrated within the
direct line of Longleat descent through their daughter, Frances, the sister of
William who died young and without issue.

For Frances Thynne went on to marry Sir Robert Worsley – and it was
their daughter Frances Worsley who married Lord Carteret (subsequently
Earl of Granville) who was the father of Louisa Carteret. There was perhaps
some poetic justice in the idea that the Longleat line did, after all, come to
descend from the 1st Viscount, through the manipulative marital arrangements of his clan.

In other ways the young couple were perhaps not quite so well
matched. Mrs Delany's own recorded verdict on Thomas was that he was
'warm in temper, for he cannot bear contradiction and has not discernment
to be reasoned with'. Yet she could not very well escape from the responsibility of having saddled sweet Louisa with this young brute, so the judgement she pushed in her direction was that he was 'affectionate and good
natured'. Someone who expressed herself rather more bluntly was Sarah,
Duchess of Marlborough who, when writing to her grand-daughter,
lamented that the 'agreeable' Louisa should be marrying 'such a pig'. And
the poor girl was only nineteen years old.

The 2nd Viscount's idea of the fit use of Longleat was as a hunting
ground. Lord and Lady Landsdown had already permitted the ornate gar-

dens to degenerate into little better than a tangled scrubland, and some of it he now turned back into pasture land. He had always been an accomplished horseman, for it was all part of becoming 'a young noblemen' (the image that had been foisted upon him as a child). His hunting activities as a young man are portrayed in the huge set of paintings by Wooton, which he commissioned to hang in the Great Hall. His supercilious and arrogantly pouting face peers down from the walls of Longleat far more frequently than has come to be regarded as his due.

Marriage and fatherhood wrought their benefit upon Thomas, for Louisa evidently brought out the best in him. He even started paying attention to the needs of Longleat and its tenants, although his special imprint upon the environment was limited to the laying down of a front drive between an avenue of elm trees (now replaced by tulip trees). The young couple also spent much of the year in their London house, where Louisa was held socially in high esteem.

Of their relationship Mrs Delany noted: 'He is excessively fond of her, which I do not wonder at, for if anyone's heart is to be won by merit, she has a good title to his. I never saw more complaisance and sweetness of manner than she has in her whole behaviour.' As for Thomas, Mrs Delany wrote that his time was mis-spent. He was impressionable, inclined to drink, and 'easily worked on by those who have his ear'.

But if this period is to be regarded as the happiest within a sad life, it wasn't to endure for long. After giving birth to a third son within four years of marriage, Louisa's health deteriorated suddenly, and on Christmas Day 1736 she died, leaving Thomas 'like a madman' (as Mrs Delany records).

According to family legend, Louisa's ghost still haunts Longleat. Thomas had become insanely jealous of one of his employees at Longleat (or so the story runs), supposing the man to be Louisa's secret lover. I should perhaps interject at this point that the 2nd Viscount was of notoriously poor judgement, and so could have been prone to believe any tittle-tattle that was whispered in his ear by those who stood to advantage themselves from the servant's dismissal. But it would have been in character for Thomas, under such circumstances, to have flown into a blind rage. According to the legend, in any case, the faithless retainer was murdered by being flung down the spiral staircase that descends from the top passage within the East Wing of the house. It is up on that top passage that the beautiful Louisa is said still to be searching for her vanished 'lover'.

A lady in green or grey (the tale is flexible)

treks the eternal circuit of the upper floor,
ignoring assured statements from solemn faces
that the places are empty – the devoted servant fled.
Her tread animates the creaking passage boards
from a store of blended (if loosely remembered) legends,
to register atmosphere more real than the pallid
reality, within his palace of squabbling unrest.
Her zest for life had wilted on its wizened stem,
as trembling doubts paraded possibilities,
filling her youthful well-instructed head
with dread perception of permanent marital bonds.
Within that troubled brood where she belonged,
she feared the worst, on sensing drastic wrong.

My feeling is that it would be curious if this man's direct descendants
(amongst whom I myself am numbered) had seen fit to concoct such a legend unless there were some truth in it. And it is interesting to note that in
1915, when a boiler for central heating was first installed at Longleat, the
workmen down in the cellars uncovered beneath the flagstones a skeleton
wearing jackboots dateable to this period. The remains were then placed
within a hatbox (as I've been told), and quietly interred within
Horningsham churchyard.

Whatever the reason, Thomas was so much turned against the thought
of continuing to live at Longleat after the death of Louisa that he took his
brood of three young children, plus the aged nanny, and moved to a small
house in Horningsham (opposite the contemporary war memorial) quite
inconsolable, as Mrs Delany liked to think. As for Longleat itself, it was
emptied, the windows shuttered, and the entire domestic staff dismissed,
for he had lost all interest in the estate, which now plunged heavily into
both debt and disrepair.

His stable (including racehorses) was perhaps all that kept his interest
in Wiltshire alive, although up in London he was not without achievement
and esteem. He was Grand Master of the Freemasons, Keeper of Hyde
Park, Ranger of St James's Park and Keeper of the Mall – not that any
of these posts might have been said to furnish him with his prime interests
in life.

Then finally in 1751, at the age of forty-one, he died, arranging in his
will that he should not be laid to rest in the family vault at Longbridge
Deverill. Instead of that (and with certain retrospective poetic justice per-

haps), he was buried in the same churchyard at Horningsham where the remains of the mystery corpse were also, at a later date, to join him.

If my judgement upon the 2nd Viscount be too harsh, let me now soften it by quoting a poem, found amongst his papers and probably composed by himself – unless we should suppose that it was some favourite verse by another, which he copied out in his own hand. Let us give him the benefit of the doubt, in which case there may have been a sensitive (if troubled) soul concealed beneath those petulant features. It might even seem that he was aware that he had led a wasted, if exalted, life, where death itself is the final leveller.

> Can costly robes or beds of down,
> can all the gems that deck the fair,
> can all the glories of the crown,
> give health or ease the brow of care?
>
> The sceptred king, the burdened slave,
> the humble and the haughty die.
> The great, the good, the just, the brave,
> in dust without distinction lie.

# Chapter 4

## Ancestry: The general picture

### The Eighteenth & Nineteenth Centuries

### THOMAS THYNNE, THE 1ST MARQUESS OF BATH (1734-1796)

The 2nd Viscount's two surviving sons were named – you'll never guess! – Thomas, and Henry Frederick. But it is only the former who should concern us here. He was eighteen when he succeeded his father as the 3rd Viscount Weymouth, and at twenty-one he took the decision to move back into Longleat. This was in 1754. He was charming, ambitious but lazy, and on an even more dubious note, he was to be described later as a man of unprincipled cunning.

During these early years there may also have been some doubts concerning his sexual orientation. George II commented that he could not be 'a good kind of man', since he was never seen in the company of women: the gaming tables and the drinking of strong beer in the company of his fellow-men were all that he appeared to enjoy. And Lady Caroline Fox observed dryly that he was 'a very pretty man' – for which his descendants should be grateful, since it meant that Louisa's (rather than her husband's) looks had been genetically transmitted within the main line of the Thynne family.

On the question of sexuality, at the age of twenty-six Thomas set the record straight by marrying Lady Elizabeth Cavendish-Bentinck, the twenty-five-year-old daughter of the Duke of Portland, by whom he had children frequently. In retrospect, it was regarded as a happy marriage despite there being so much publicised infidelity on his side.

The 3rd Viscount launched himself with some extravagance into the task of bringing Longleat back into good repair, both the house and the grounds. But the fashion in landscape had now turned away from ornate gardens such as had been introduced by the 1st Viscount, towards the romantic idea of enhanced natural settings. The task of transforming the Longleat landscape was entrusted to Capability Brown, so as to enfold the house within its park, as if the one really belonged to the other. Huge quantities of earth were displaced and resituated, all by hand. The shape of the leat was changed, although not into the form that we know today, and the empty scrubland became woodland plantation, surrounding the rolling pastureland of the park, with Longleat as the jewel at its centre.

Within this new pastoral setting, the young household developed idyllic ways. A grotto was built to house an imported hermit who, in return for his stipend, had to dress in sackcloth, with both hair and fingernails uncut, refusing to answer when addressed by any of the Longleat employees. But it is recorded that he debunked from his post and was later found drinking in a Warminster tavern. There were also fun and games near by the hermit's grotto, involving a ring of small boulders reminiscent of Stonehenge – for dancing, in all probability, as if the ring furnished some kind of maypole. But an exact description of such merriment has not survived.

Thomas' political career began to take off when George III came to the throne in 1760. It was only then that he received his first official post, as Lord of the Bedchamber. He then became associated with the fourth Duke of Bedford and the influential group known as the Bloomsbury Gang, containing members of the landed Whig aristocracy who dominated political life during the early years of the King's reign. But his taste for gambling, in addition to the landscaping of Longleat's park, brought him near to bankruptcy, so that some kind of official remuneration for his work became more than just desirable. And through Bedford's influence, in 1765, he was offered the vacant post of Secretary of State for Ireland, pocketed the year's salary of £19,000, and promptly resigned – without ever having actually visited the place, and despite owning a large estate out there.

When he next held office, in 1768, it was as Secretary of State for the North. He was transferred later that year to being Secretary of State for the South, just at the time when John Wilkes was causing trouble and London was threatened with mob rule. Thomas thus became responsible for the maintenance of law and order, a task to which he was ill-suited, being of too indolent a disposition. So in 1770 he seized an opportunity to resign, in that he found himself the only member of the cabinet in favour of declaring war against Spain in a dispute over the ownership of the Falkland Islands.

By 1775 he was back as Secretary of State with special concern for the North American colonies. This was just after he had acquired a vast estate of 700,000 acres (283,300 hectares) in North Carolina, bequeathed to him by his Carteret uncle, Earl Granville, since Louisa's brother had finally died without an heir. But with the disaffection of the settlers in that state, he never managed to get his ownership of the land properly authenticated. Nor could George III or his Prime Minister, Lord North, furnish any assistance because between the three of them they had already alienated the American colonies, culminating in their Declaration of Independence. They were all in this business together, however, so they had few reproaches to offer one another.

On finding himself with debts in excess of £25,000, Thomas was persuaded to give more of his time to the efficient management of the Longleat estate, which necessitated that he should extricate himself completely from politics. He had served under Grenville, Rockingham, Grafton and North, but he had never scintillated as a minister, and had certainly drawn the fire of some of the government's enemies. He was the first member of the Thynne family to get pilloried in the gutter press (by Junius, amongst others), mainly as a gambling debauchee who was too fond of his claret, burgundy and port, but also because of an affair with Harriet Lambe, a noted courtesan. Despite all this he had acquired for himself a certain public respect as an astute parliamentarian, who was once described as a prompt and graceful speaker: 'though to profit by the latter it was necessary to follow him to White's, to drink of claret, and to remain at table to a very late hour of the night'.

On hearing of his intended resignation, George III endeavoured without success to persuade him to soldier on for a few years. This was in 1789, a year when in France at least people were having second thoughts about the value of aristocracy. But the King now decided to reward the fifty-six-year-old Viscount by conferring upon him a Marquisate – the marquesses being largely a Hanoverian innovation, introduced within the hierarchy of the British peerage so as to remain lesser in aristocratic standing to the dukes and yet superior to the politically troublesome earls. They were a new breed of noblemen, powerful, and yet of relatively recent rise to national distinction.

To bring Thomas' career to its social zenith, George III and Queen Charlotte came to spend two nights at Longleat. They were feasted and paraded before a loyally carousing throng in a pageantry such as Longleat had not seen since the visit of Queen Elizabeth I. And before his departure the King was heard to remark that 'everything at Longleat is very good.'

So Thomas now became known as the 1st Marquess of Bath, and he passed the final seven years of his life predominantly at Longleat, endeavouring to get the finances of the estate into good working order. And as an initial gesture of a reformed lifestyle, he sold off the contents of his wine cellar.

His interests were still wide, as can be noted for example in his collection of telescopes and scientific instruments which are still preserved in the house. But his main concern was for agricultural improvement. He even received an award from the Bath Agricultural Society for his research to discover which breed of sheep are best suited to the pastures of the West Country. The woodlands that he had planted some thirty years earlier were just beginning to take shape, and the farms were now profitable. The mortgages taken out by the 2nd Viscount were all repaid, but his own extravagance in matters of modernisation necessitated a new loan, this time for the considerable sum of £80,000.

His health was also failing as the years of dissipation began to take their toll, and the use of a sedan chair was forced upon him by his gout. On a visit to London in 1796, he died. A 700-man mounted escort returned his corpse to Longleat, and he was buried in the family vault at Longbridge Deverill. If he had failed to obtain any real political success, he had still succeeded in rescuing the estate from near ruin, and he left behind him the new woodlands, Capability Brown's park landscape, nine children, his title – and his debts.

## THOMAS THYNNE,
## THE 2ND MARQUESS OF BATH (1765-1837)

The 2nd Marquess of Bath, who was once again called Thomas, inherited when he was thirty-one years old. He was a far shyer man than his father, less sure of himself, perhaps, but free from excesses in either gambling or drinking habits. He was married to a plump, homely, jovial woman – Isabella Byng, the daughter of Viscount Torrington – who bore him eleven children, some of whom were to give cause for embarrassment.

But I'll be coming to all that later.

Isabella made it her special concern to involve herself with the estate tenants, devising schemes to improve their conditions, while Thomas applied his attention to the task of completing, or rebuilding, the parts of Longleat that had been left incomplete in the sixteenth century, refashioning portions of the garden and park, and generally consolidating the estate after his father's life of extravagance. Not that he himself stinted on spending money where he deemed it necessary. By the year 1815, for example, he had paid out more than £100,000 upon the rebuilding programme. And the increased levels of taxation (to finance the Napoleonic Wars) no doubt made life difficult for him and his family. But the fact remains that by the time of his death, the estate had been set back into good order.

So let us examine what he did. Most of it, indeed, can be described in terms of what both Jeffrey Wyatt and Humphrey Repton (separately) constructed, on Thomas' commission. A North Wing was added to the house so as to enclose two courtyards. A system of corridors was also introduced so as to lessen the dependence upon room-to-room entry or exit. And the walls of each bedroom were decorated with hand-painted Chinese wallpaper towards the end of the century – probably predating what rapidly became a fashion, once the Prince Regent had introduced such decor into his Brighton Pavilion. A grand front staircase appeared, replacing a smaller spiral one by Sir Christopher Wren, which the 1st Viscount had commissioned, while coal stoves, branched candelabra, and flushing water closets were included in the bathrooms for the first time.

The former assortment of stable buildings were replaced with a stable courtyard more akin to the character of the house. An arching South Lodge was constructed at the head of the front drive, and a Gothic Lodge to act as a boathouse upon the new lake at Shearwater, which was now filled with water, although the Warminster common land comprising its original basin had originally been enclosed by the 1st Marquess. The meandering river, or leat, such as had been left by Capability Brown, was now resculpted into a series of lakes with a waterfall, and a boathouse was introduced at the bottom of the garden. A picnic area was also laid out upon a newly cleared hill summit, which they entitled Heaven's Gate.

Within the category of interests and hobbies, Thomas was concerned to carry on the traditions of the house. He acquired valuable items of furniture, and added to his father's collection of scientific instruments. He also collected first editions for the library, if somewhat indiscriminately, without any special theme. Isabella was of a more literary turn of mind, and as the unlikely aristocratic disciple of William Cobbett (who was after all a distinctly Radical MP) she published a selection of his writings on self-sufficiency, presenting a copy to each of the cottagers on the estate.

This was an age when the social structure of Britain had been undergoing much rapid change as it geared itself for the Industrial Revolution. But it was the practice of enclosing such common land as was only lightly farmed by the local community which had deprived many people of their livelihood. The custom of enclosing land in this way had been widespread over the past century, and the Longleat estate had no doubt profited from all this, but not so their tenants. There may have been increased opportunities for employment upon the estate, but Thomas and Isabella perceived how the ties between house and local community ought to be strengthened psychologically.

Picnicking was therefore encouraged within the estate grounds, and Longleat itself was, for the first time, thrown open to the public once a week and free of charge. Indeed, there is a family legend that the 2nd Marquess was once revealed in hiding when an inquisitive tourist made too personal an investigation into what some cupboard might contain. But the will existed to benefit others, and to be esteemed thereby. So he was probably an excellent choice in his appointment as Lord Lieutenant of Somerset. And in 1823, his career peaked when he was created a Knight of the Garter, although some peers were dismayed that he should thus have been singled out for such distinction after what had been a fairly quiet, if sober, life.

His later years had in fact been troubled by the behaviour of his sons. Two of his daughters were to marry just as he might have hoped, to the Earl of Harewood and to the Duke of Buccleuch. But in 1820, and without consulting either parent, his twenty-four-year-old son and heir (Thomas, the 5th Viscount Weymouth) eloped to the continent with Harriet Robbins, the black-haired and beautiful daughter of the local tollkeeper. The Marquess was furious at this disruption of the family harmony, and, indeed, at the affront to the whole family's decorum and respectability.

A certain inflexibility in parental posture had suddenly raised its ugly head. For two months there was complete silence, but eventually a letter from Italy arrived, in which the young Weymouth wrote:

> You know the remorse I feel for having given so many mis-
> eries to so good a father ... A sort of fate hurried us on ... I
> saw myself surrounded by misfortunes which I find at last
> were of my own making ... My mind was in a state of con-
> fusion and despair, and I am ashamed to say I tried to attach
> the blame on you. I did not dare open the last letter from
> you for a long time, but when I did, I flew to anything to
> drive away reflection ...

Weymouth had already blotted his copybook even before Harriet Robbins
had captivated his heart, having almost got himself imprisoned for debt;
his reputation for drunkenness might further indicate that he had inherited his grandfather's vices without perhaps his abilities. But formalising this
'discreditable connexion' by marrying Harriet was regarded as the last straw
to the breaking of the relationship between father and son. It caused a rup-
ture that was never to mend, despite some favourable reports concerning
how the young marrieds were faring.

It was the Marquess's wish to exclude his eldest son from the Longleat
succession. Money was even offered to get Weymouth to relinquish his heritage. But it was declined with the assertion that they were happy to bide
their time living in Paris, where they had finally settled, until his father
died and Longleat would be theirs, to use as they pleased. And by the terms
of the family entail, Weymouth had the law on his side, no matter what his
father might threaten.

Of his younger sons, there were two – Charles and Edward – who
caused some additional embarrassment to the family, principally by their
debts, causing the 2nd Marquess to send a notice to the *Times*, disclaiming
all responsibility for their insolvency. There is no clear record of what
became of these brothers, but it is possible that Charles may have ended up
in Canada and Edward in Australia, inasmuch that there now appear to be
distant Thynne 'cousins' on both of those continents, claiming recent
descent from the Longleat Thynnes – although there would seem to be no
record of such emigrations within the family archives. So the relationship
may possibly be more distant.

Isabella had striven in vain to keep the family united, being the only
one in the family to travel to Paris to stay with the Viscount and
Viscountess. Before leaving, she forgave them for their 'unkindness and
misconduct'. But as far as her husband was concerned, it was all to no avail.
And after Isabella's death in 1830, there was no one left to help bridge the

gulf between father and son. In fact, the whole sense of unity within the family began to disintegrate, both the Marquess and his heir hanging on to their lives in a determination to outlive the other.

If the 2nd Marquess may have been too stern and rigid as a father, I must quote from the letter which Isabella had delivered to him after her death, and which speaks well for his role as husband. She wrote:

> I cannot bear the idea of being snatched away from this world without bearing some testimony to the affection that has entirely filled my heart for my beloved husband. Accept my grateful thanks for all the kindness and happiness you have bestowed on me for so many years, which has been returned by the warmest affection that one mortal is capable of for another. ... Talk to our children of your interests, of your affairs, and try to get reacquainted with theirs. Be their friend, as well as their respected father ...

She wrote those last sentences with the understanding, perhaps, that the family unity was crumbling, and that with her gone, it would soon fall apart.

In the event, the 2nd Marquess did manage to outlive his son, the 5th Viscount, but only by the skin of his teeth – by a matter of five weeks, in fact. He himself was seventy-four when he died, and Weymouth a mere forty-one, with Harriet just a few years younger than that when she became a widow. So the family now awaited with bated breath to hear if she were pregnant. Insensitive suggestions were made about getting her to submit to an official examination so as to preclude the possibility of her turning up at Longleat in years to come, having acquired a son of approximately the right age, to claim the inheritance retrospectively.

Yet such cynicism proved unwarranted. Harriet went on to marry an Italian nobleman, and never did have any children. But in any case she did not attempt, nor wish, to give any further trouble to the Thynne family.

> Accustomed as you **were** to **rid**ing **rough**shod on the **black**
> **track** of your **pamp**ered **whims**, you **lost** your **heart**
> to the **artful charms** of a **loc**al **coun**try **girl** –
> then **hurled** your **fortune** to the **wind** in **hasty flight**.
> **Fright**ening, implac**able** in his **wound**ed **pride**, your **fath**er
> would **rath**er **lose** an **errant son** than accept

his inept and socially demeaning marital bond,
responding in wrath with threats of disinheritance.
The terrible ticking of calendrical clocks told
of the old man ageing, but holding it back
with unslackening grit in a mutual determination
to motion the other first to the life hereafter.
Although you hoped that time was on your side,
by early death your dreams were nullified.

## HENRY FREDERICK THYNNE, THE 3RD MARQUESS OF BATH (1797-1837)

The 2nd Marquess was succeeded by his second son, who had been christened (what else?) Henry Frederick. Not a great deal has been left on record about the 3rd Marquess, but he was forty at the time he inherited, and was married to Harriet Baring, the daughter of Baron Ashburton, with two sons to reinforce the family's hopes that the dynasty might continue. He had spent most of his life in the Royal Navy, at one time commanding the sloop *Frolic*. Other commands followed, and he saw active service in the Mediterranean and South Atlantic. He was a sober, fair-minded and competent captain, but little more can be said than just that.

He had never expected to inherit Longleat, so had rarely visited the place. And now that he found it to be his own, he admitted to feeling uncomfortable there. But in any case, within three months of the 2nd Marquess's dying, he himself was dead, leaving his eldest six-year-old son to inherit Longleat, under the prolonged tutelage of the Dowager 3rd Marchioness.

# Chapter 5

## Ancestry: The general picture

### The end of the Nineteenth Century

## JOHN ALEXANDER THYNNE,
## THE 4TH MARQUESS OF BATH (1831-1896)

John Alexander, the 4th Marquess of Bath, became known by the second of his forenames – Alexander being a family name of the Barings. And it should be appreciated that now, once again, as had happened before when Lady Landsdown was bringing up the 2nd Viscount, a mother who had been widowed relatively young found herself responsible for tutoring the heir to Longleat according to a cultural pattern of her own choosing. The Baring as opposed to the Thynne character therefore may well have been emphasised. But the 4th Marquess was old enough when his father died to retain some personal memory of him, and there were numerous uncles and aunts who, on their visits, were no doubt concerned to keep the Thynne traditions very much alive. The fact that Harriet Baring never saw fit to remarry is indicative that she may have preferred to identify herself within the Thynne family mould.

She had in fact displayed admirable competence and financial restraint in her management of the estates, with the assistance of various agents. There were all together three estates at this time: at Longleat, in Shropshire and in Ireland. And by the time of Alexander's coming of age, there was more than £50,000 in the kitty. An additional point about Harriet is that, for the first time, she introduced a gene of substantial longevity into the Thynne family, finally dying in 1892 at the age of eighty-eight – a revered Victorian Dowager Marchioness, residing at Munpham Court in Sussex over the latter half of her life.

The 4th Marquess was by all accounts shy (like his grandfather), a disposition attributable no doubt to the isolating nature of an upbringing at Longleat. There is a description of him by Thackeray, who met him in Paris while still a very young man, as a high-bred, high-fed, petted and not over-wise young-man-about-town, whose greatest religion was brandy and water. But then intellectuals of Thackeray's calibre do somewhat delight in the chance to demean those categories in society which have impressed upon them their unreasoned access to life's opportunities.

Alex (as he was more usually called) was in fact well educated – at Eton and Cambridge – of good intellectual standing and of high Christian principles. He was to be described in his obituary, many years later, as a highly cultured, scrupulously honest English gentleman of the best type, who remained unto the last under a cloak of reserve bordering upon hauteur, but one of the most kind-hearted of men.

A characteristic in which he seems to have made some progress on his forebears was in his appreciation of art, developing a fervent admiration for the Italian Renaissance. This dated from his Grand Tour of Europe as a young man, although it was to be some years before it bore any fruit. Then deeming that Longleat was itself a building of that inspiration, he decided (in the fashion of many other Victorians) to imitate such a historical style of decor when refurbishing his home. He then embarked upon the construction of his dream interiors for Longleat, with a vision at heart of the palatial splendours he had viewed when in Italy.

Alex was thirty before he married. His bride was Frances (Fanny) Vesey, the daughter of Viscount de Vesci, and reports varied concerning whether it was to be regarded as a good match. A friend of the family commented that his marriage to Frances would ruin the finest brains in Britain. Perhaps he was really just trying to say that she was shallow. But someone else found her high-minded and charming. Disraeli after two visits to the house – which he found profoundly gloomy – had words of commendation for his hostess, however, appreciating her gay, light-hearted good humour. And his comment upon Alexander, when in her company, was that he had never met a man so entirely absorbed in the existence of another.

Petite and elegant, her numerous dresses are still preserved at Longleat. In many ways she was, in character, the exact opposite of her husband, being witty and gregarious in contrast to his cool solemnity. Fanny's vivacity was perhaps the best possible antidote to Alex's own instinct for solitude. By encouraging impromptu house parties, dinners and outings, she saved him from fastidiousness and persuaded him to change his habits.

There had been a time when she had her doubts about the prospect of marrying him, being someone who carefully vetted those who were courting her. She once wrote to a friend about another suitor: 'I want to know if he has family diamonds and much plate.' And she nearly married Lord Longford, shortly prior to her marrying Alex. Subsequent generations of both Pakenhams and Thynnes can be thankful that she finally decided against that match, in that their very existence today depends upon the genetic selection having been precisely as it turned out to be, after their second thoughts on the issue. But in any case it would appear that Fanny was well pleased with her final choice, in that she wrote to her mother shortly after returning from their honeymoon, to say: 'I am so happy with Bath. His good qualities come out more and more every day.'

The year when Alex inherited Longleat was 1837, coinciding with the accession of Victoria to the throne – and he was to die in 1896, just five years short of the Queen. The entire period can therefore be regarded as eminently Victorian, with the dignity and pursuits that would be regarded as typical of that age.

Significant too was the pomp and snobbery which now emerged as an important character of life amongst the family's servants and retainers below stairs. Now that the middle classes in Britain had become so important, and conscious of their own identity, the residual aristocracy (alongside the monarchy) had their own sense of identity delineated for them by the new social groups. An acceptance of the prevailing class divisions was taken for granted within Longleat's enlarged domestic household. Who was entitled to speak to whom, and with what degree of informality was all carefully regulated within what came to be regarded as standard etiquette, and literature on the subject soon rigidified the rules still further. Yet within that household, everyone knew his or her place, and much of the nostalgia within my parents' own generation found its inspiration here, in what they grew up regarding as a golden age for Longleat.

Alex is perhaps most remembered for his introduction of the Italianate decor (as previously mentioned) within all the grand rooms on the East Wing of the house. But he also added his own collection of books to the library, having taken the French Revolution as his particular theme. In this and many other ways he certainly left his mark on the place. And it was here that he entertained many famous guests, including royalty. For example, the Prince of Wales and Princess Alexandra were at Longleat for four days in 1881 for a shooting party.

The 4th Marquess was thought to furnish the social centre of life in the West Country, in terms of being the tone-setter for those who wished to live decorously. While having been raised upon the Victorian ethos of duty, responsibility and self-improvement, he was relaxed to the point of shyness in his approach to such matters, always preferring his home life, interspersed with bouts of foreign travel, to any more determinedly ambitious goals.

It was his love of privacy which prevented him from really entering politics, although he did write an influential pamphlet on the situation in the Balkans. He also served as a special royal legate to foreign courts, on occasions when the Queen demanded such services of him, and he was appointed the Chairman of the Wiltshire County Council when it first came into existence. In addition to all this, he was an Honorary Colonel in the Wiltshire Rifle Volunteers, and a Trustee of the British Museum and the National Portrait Gallery.

Alex had seen Longleat's prosperity reach its peak, and begin to decline. The years of agricultural depression had turned the scales of fortune against landed estates in favour of the new industrial empires, and in his awareness of what was taking place within the country, he became morose and unsociable. Moreover, someone described him as being preternaturally thin and singularly pedantic in his mannerisms. He had little faith in the ability of his eldest son, Thomas, to maintain Longleat and was pessimistic about the future of England and its empire.

It was during a final bout of travelling abroad, to get away from it all, that Alexander (at the age of sixty-five) finally died, and his body was returned to England for burial within the family vault at Longbridge Deverill. Fanny survived him, to continue the recent family tradition of living as a revered Dowager Marchioness, offering encouragement and wisdom in the background. Harriet, the 3rd Marchioness, had prepared a new Dowager suite in the West Wing for her own use whenever revisiting Longleat – decorated with Chinese wallpaper similar to, if more recent than, the ones previously installed upstairs. And it was now Fanny's turn to have substantial use of this suite. She was to die much later during the First World War.

# THOMAS THYNNE,
## THE 5TH MARQUESS OF BATH (1862-1946)

Of the six children fathered by the 4th Marquess, three had been sons, named with almost complete predictability Thomas, John and Alexander. If there had been a fourth, there could be little doubt that he would have been called Henry Frederick. Yet John was in fact killed in a riding accident while still a young man, and of the two surviving brothers, Alexander was by far the most extrovertly sociable, remaining a popular womanising bachelor until his death in action in 1918. So it was Thomas alone of this particular generation (which is to say, the eldest brother and 5th Marquess of Bath) upon whom rested all hope of sustaining a direct line from their father. Alternatively, the line would pass through the descendants of Alex's brother, Ulrick Thynne. The need for a son and heir to survive the gauntlet of life had always been a worry within the family.

Of Thomas' three sisters, there was Alice who was to marry Sir Hugh Shaw Stewart, a wiry little man with a brittle temper. 'Bosh, Alice!' he was often heard to say when his wife was expounding her views. My mother describes her as having a curious Thynne family trait (shared to some extent by Thomas) of taking a deep breath and rolling her eyes upwards until nothing but the whites could be seen, while at the same time fluttering her eyelids, and using this to emphasise any point she wished to make. She also displayed a tendency to pouch her food in her cheeks, like a monkey, unpouching it again later for digestion at her leisure.

The second sister was Katie, who was to marry Lord Cromer of Egypt. She was sweet and gentle, but was bullied by the other sisters – as a result of which she steered her own serene course.

Finally there was Beatrice, who never married and was the only one of my great-aunts to survive into my own day. She had been an art student at the Slade, and was painted on several occasions by Henry Tonks. Some say she was romantically involved with him as well. She was certainly the most eccentric, and perhaps the most intellectual, of the sisters. Virginia Woolf was fascinated by Beatrice and thought she possessed 'not only rank, beauty and easy pleasant good manners but a kind of lazy pagan majesty, a natural grace'. These qualities were no longer quite so visible by the time I knew her. But she was the only artist within recent generations on either side of my family.

The relationship between Thomas and his father had never been close. The 4th Marquess had mistrusted his son's reserve, describing it as 'the evil he most has to combat', and Thomas' 'strange reluctance to open his mind' made his father unwilling to involve him in the running of the estate during his own lifetime.

Educated at Eton and Bailliol College, Oxford, Thomas grew up shy, independent and self-reliant. After a period of travelling abroad, he returned to England and entered Parliament as the Conservative member for Frome, eventually in 1905 to serve briefly as Secretary of State for Ireland. But he was to become better known locally as the Chairman of the Wiltshire County Council, a post which he held for nearly forty years. In 1922 he was created Lord Lieutenant of Somerset, and, finally, some years later, a Knight of the Garter, which marked the summit of his career. Only the 2nd Marquess had previously been rewarded with such high honour – but the reason for it, in the case of the 5th Marquess, was supposed in part to be his personal contribution to the war effort in 1914, when he turned Longleat into a hospital for the convalescence of those wounded at the front (running it largely at his own expense), and in part to be his close personal relationship with the royal family.

Back in the 1880s when Thomas was still a very young man, it had been planned that he should marry the beautiful Princess Mary of Teck, who was then in London completing her education. Being so shy a person, however, Thomas gave her insufficient indication that this might still be the intention he had in mind. In fact, against all the wishes of his parents, he had fallen in love with the frail and mysterious Violet Moncrieffe, whose very birth had been a matter of considerable social scandal.

More on that in a moment.

But Thomas didn't know how to deal with the problem of not proposing to the lady his parents so much anticipated would become their daughter-in-law. His solution was to go abroad – and he remained there until Princess Mary had fallen in love with someone else, who happened to be none other than the future King George V. So the story had a happy ending for both parties, in that Thomas now felt free to return from his travels, to plead more strongly for his parents' acceptance of the lady who had captured his heart. As for Queen Mary (to call her by her subsequent name), she became a life-long friend of my grandfather, and he remained a trusted counsellor and representative of the Crown within the West Country at large.

The enigma surrounding the birth of the lady whom Thomas was eventually to marry is of course of particular interest to me, in that I am descended from her genes. My grandmother was the daughter of Harriet Moncrieffe, who married Sir Charles Maudant, a close friend of the Prince of Wales. But after Violet's birth in 1869, Lady Maudant told her husband that he was not the father. In fact, she went a lot further by confessing that there had been a number of lovers and that she had 'done wrong' (as she put it) 'with the Prince of Wales, often and in open day'. The name she had mentioned with the greatest degree of affection was that of Lord Cole, who later became the 4th Earl of Enniskillen. But she also named Sir Frederic Johnstone, who had left her if not with child, then most probably with the venereal infection which she had acquired at this time. And her list included the Prince of Wales, with an additional three names also mentioned, some of which were not quite grand enough to merit official inclusion. But the net result was that Sir Charles started divorce proceedings against his wife in what became known as 'the Warwickshire scandal'.

Now it wasn't the custom in Victorian days to drag royalty through the divorce courts, but here was someone saying that the Queen's own son and heir had been guilty of adultery. Apart from Lady Maudant's own confession, letters and a valentine in the Prince's handwriting were found amongst her papers, and Sir Charles' servants swore that the Prince had visited Lady Maudant regularly when her husband was out of the house. When such evidence was disclosed, the whole nation was duly shocked.

Sir Charles was in fact restrained from citing the Prince as a co-respondent. To contend with the lady's own testimony, it was rapidly decided that she was insane, and merely fantasising upon her relationship with the Prince. She ended her days suitably castigated by Victorian ethics, locked away in an asylum. As for the rest, the Prince was called to give evidence, and recited a carefully rehearsed negation to a series of short questions, to the effect that there had never been any 'improper familiarity or criminal act' between himself and Lady Maudant. The focus of attention was then permitted to shift towards Viscount Cole, who had indeed been cited, and who avoided the requirement of perjuring himself by going on a prolonged trip abroad. But the secret concerning who my great-grandfather truly was remains uncertain to this day, an extensive analysis of the DNA of the descendants of all the parties concerned being now perhaps the only method by which such a question could be resolved.

It was in 1890 that Thomas and Violet were married, when he was twenty-eight and she herself was twenty-one. And just four years later, at the death of the 4th Marquess, they moved into Longleat as the new master and mistress. There was a London house in Grosvenor Square which accounted for some of their time, but it was at Longleat where they mostly lived, and their residence there was to span the reigns of both Edward VII and George V.

The Irish estate had already been sold by the 4th Marquess, in his final years, to compensate for the loss in agricultural revenue elsewhere. The Thynnes had been absentee landlords at Carrickmacross, and despite an extensive charitable programme that had been implemented from time to time, their departure from the Irish scene cannot have been lamented. And Thomas himself was to sell off the Shropshire estate immediately after the First World War, to compensate once again for the declining revenue from the Longleat estate.

In one respect, however, Thomas set the estate upon a highly lucrative course. He took the decision to participate in the commercial exploitation of the Cheddar caves. It was not an idea that originated from himself, in that the tourist attractions were already a going concern. The two caves had in fact been discovered during the life of the 4th Marquess, the first in 1837 by a miller called Mr Cox, who had been quarrying for limestone to build himself a carthouse when he had broken through into what is now known as Cox's cave. And right from the start, Cox had charged an admission fee to any tourist who expressed a curiosity to view the splendid array of stalactites and stalagmites that it contained. Then during the 1880s he had tried to sell the cave, but was prevented from doing so when the Thynne family's lawyers pointed out that it was the legal property of the man who owned the farmland up above – who happened to be the 4th Marquess.

Then the second cave was discovered by Mr Gough, a local entrepreneur who had long been probing around in the gorge in the hopes of making such a discovery and then exploiting it. Considerable excavation was taking place during the 1890s, despite the fact that it had now been legally established where the ownership lay. He was, however, permitted to exploit the commercial potential of Gough's cave in the same manner that Mr Cox was permitted to continue in the presentation of the other one. The sum of one shilling and sixpence was demanded of tourists in those days – which, it should be noted, was in fact a sizeable proportion of the current average weekly wage.

No doubt there had originally been some resistance to the idea of the Thynne family's participating in so blatantly a commercial venture. But the caves were now attracting the major public interest they deserved. They had been carved out from the soft limestone crags by the melting ice which swirled through the gorge in an underground torrent during five successive Ice Ages. And there was additional public interest when the remains of a skeleton were unearthed in 1903 from a hollow cavity just a little way inside the entrance of Gough's cave. These bones were eventually to be dated as coming from the Palaeolithic age, some 9,000 years ago. They were promptly put on display to the visiting public as the earliest of human remains ever yet discovered in the British Isles. And it was around this time that Thomas took these enterprises under his own wing, employing relatives of the Gough and Cox families to run them for him.

The commercial exploitation was low-key, but still it represented a start. He had taken the plunge, so to speak, by displaying a willingness (now that his father was safely deceased) to indulge in commerce. And it might be said that the business interests of the Longleat estate were thenceforward geared towards tourism and what were ultimately to be described as the leisure industries.

Violet was a brand of Marchioness somewhat different from her predecessors, coming from a more risqué demi-mondaine background. Her uncertain parental identity may have coloured her own constant quest for identity with the Deity – a search for God that culminated in her adoption of the Christian Scientists' faith. She was someone who set great store by her personal visions concerning events that were still to happen. ('Pictures before my eyes', as she chose to describe them.) And her children grew up revering what came to be known as her psychic powers.

To some extent she was a lonely figure, never fully coming to terms with the innumerable Thynnes who flooded through Longleat: cousins, great-uncles and nieces all being equally welcome. Violet lacked their sense of family unity and kinship. She took refuge in her religion, writing copious notes on the character of Christ and the meaning of the Lord's Prayer. Amongst her papers is an enigmatic letter that suggests her sense of isolation went far deeper than anyone realised. It was written to her by a friend with whom she had shared a railway compartment on a journey across France, shortly before the start of the First World War.

> The situation is this, we have mutually fallen in love with each other. If I had been a man, it would have been disastrous, but both being muddled women we are doing nobody any harm and ourselves, I think, a great deal of good, as we

are able to give what the other lacks and help each other to
play the game.

Another feature of Violet's life that may be regarded as illuminating is that
she loved animals, and started the Pets' Cemetery at Longleat. Their tomb-
stones span the period of her residence at Longleat, and the tradition has
been continued right up to the present day.

Violet's health began to deteriorate after the First World War. She
could only walk with the aid of a stick, and spent much of her time in a
wheelchair or lying upon a day-bed in her drawing-room. But she nonetheless survived until 1928.

Between the years 1895 and 1905, Thomas and Violet had five children. The eldest was John, followed by my aunts Kathleen, Emma and
Mary. And finally came my father, Henry Frederick, a person who at that
stage was regarded as of no particular significance within the family hierarchy. All this was changed, however, with the carnage of the First World
War. John Alexander, the 9th Viscount Weymouth, was killed in action at
Hulluch, near Vermelles – where he lies buried.

The news came as no surprise to Violet, who had 'seen' his death in
one of her visions. The problem then was more a case of readjusting their
appreciation of the eleven-year-old Henry, who was now their sole surviving son and heir.

It hadn't seemed to matter very much before that his schoolwork was
abysmally bad, but there were now fears that he might not be able to match
up to the responsibilities that he would inherit. My father could remember
his mother taking him outside to get a good look at Longleat, and then asking him if he felt he was capable of looking after the place. Thereafter, he
would find himself gazing up at the great edifice while exclaiming:
'How can I look after you? I'll never be able to do it.' And in some essential formative manner, this prescribed injunction became the cornerstone
within the attitude-formation of the man who was eventually to become
the 6th Marquess.

My father in his own telling of the tale would admit to feelings of gross
inadequacy, as a young boy, for the task that was thus being imposed upon
him. He had not previously been encouraged to think that he was sufficiently significant a person to deserve such a status. And this character trait
of humility concerning his own human capacity was to remain with him
for life. He had no intellectual pretensions, having failed for Eton, and getting into Harrow only after his father had pulled strings – and the same

might be said, I dare say, for Christ Church, Oxford, where he was to read agriculture ... without actually sitting his final exams.

Signals that he was indeed regarded as an important human being, however, were constantly being fed to him from the moment he became the 10th Viscount Weymouth. And because he accepted unquestioningly the value of Longleat as something truly great, he accepted as a rider that, as scion of Longleat, some of it must wash off on himself. So he developed a curious blend of shy humility and ruthless arrogance, traceable perhaps to this sudden contrast in people's evaluation of his worth. And inasmuch that my father's attitude was to some extent formative on me, initially by his example and then, eventually, in terms of my reaction to it, I shall endeavour to paraphrase how he himself might have chosen to express it.

He might have said:

> Hierarchy is an essential part of life. Longleat, and all who belong in it, stand high within that hierarchy. I may not be especially bright. The entire Thynne family isn't especially bright; nor does it need to be, in that the power of Longleat is behind them. But I have my wits, and a certain flair for ingenuity, by means of which I can pull out of the bag all the tricks I need. With the help of my good looks and my charm I could get away with murder if the need should ever arise. But of course I wouldn't dream of doing anything quite so bad as that. I only trick and cheat within moderation, to an extent that enables me to get my own way – but no more than can be forgiven me. It would surprise me greatly if anyone accused me of ever having been other than gentlemanly in my conduct. But what is a gentleman, if we get down to it? Survival of the fittest is what really governs our lives. And having Longleat in the blood is a real survival factor. If Longleat were to be destroyed, or taken away from us, I don't think I'd have the will to live for very much longer.

# Chapter 6

## Ancestry: The general picture

### My immediate forebears

#### HENRY FREDERICK THYNNE,
#### THE 10TH VISCOUNT WEYMOUTH (1905–1992) &
#### DAPHNE VIVIAN (1904–1997)

We now come to the point where my father, Henry Frederick Thynne, the 10th Viscount Weymouth, met my mother Daphne Vivian, daughter of Baron Vivian. They had first met while he was still at Harrow, but it wasn't until he was at Oxford that they really became attracted to one another. This was in the environment of the Twenties – a decade when society was trying to set the memory of the recent war's carnage firmly in the past, without much noticeable concern for the storm clouds of economic bad weather that were gathering. It was a world in which the Bright Young Things danced the Charleston and the Black Bottom, mixed exotic cocktails and attended the fancy-dress parties given by Laura Corrigan, the ex-waitress widow of an American steel millionaire, who gave away jewellery and gold sock-suspenders to her guests.

Life for these people was an endless party, later to be satirised by Evelyn Waugh, who was an Oxford contemporary of my father's. (Waugh had disliked my father, and almost loved my mother, whom he regarded as his inspiration for characters like Agatha Runcible in *Vile Bodies*.) They indulged in wild public-baiting games, which were all part of the syndrome of an aristocratic generation heavily losing out to the upsurge of proletarian power – games like 'Follow-my-leader' through Selfridges in Oxford Street, climbing over counters and otherwise enraging customers and shop assistants alike. It was a lifestyle which contrasted diametrically with the dignified restraint demanded of them by Thomas and Violet, on the occasions when Henry invited Daphne to Longleat.

It comes therefore as no surprise that words of discouragement were heard when, in 1926, the young couple endeavoured to announce their engagement. Before proceeding, however, let us pause to examine briefly, the ancestry of this Daphne Vivian, who was to become my mother.

The Vivian family were of similar antiquity to the Thynnes – if we discount the latter's claim to have Norman ancestry. They were settled at Trenoweth in Cornwall during the reign of Henry VII, and later moved to Trewan. A descendant, Thomas Vivian (whose mother was a Cavell), married Lucy Glynn. Their son John Vivian, of Truro, became a Vice-Warden of the Stannaries. And it was his son, Sir Richard Hussey Vivian, who was in 1841 created the first Baron Vivian, famous in his day as being the man who led the last cavalry charge at Waterloo, which finally broke the back of Napoleon's army.

He was later appointed Equerry to George IV, ultimately with the rank of Lt-General. He married Eliza de Crespigny, and their son Hussey Crespigny, the 2nd Baron Vivian, became Lord Lieutenant of Cornwall, after a long spell of military service. He married Arabella Scott, who was in turn the daughter of Lady Arabella Brabazon, the sister of the Earl of Meath.

The next in line to succession was Hussey Crespigny the 3rd Baron Vivian, who was a diplomat – eventually to be appointed British Ambassador in Rome from 1891 to 1893. His wife, the beautiful Louisa Alice Duff, caused a certain stir in those circles by having a nervous breakdown while they were still in office. But she was more or less restored to good health by Dr Axel Munthe, and was able to return to her maternal duties in raising a large family, amongst whom was my maternal grandfather, George Crespigny Brabazon the 4th Baron Vivian.

George (by my mother's account) was a fierce eccentric, with a bullying streak and a love of practical jokes. At Eton he had rowed in the VIII, and had been elected into Pop. He had then embarked upon a military career, serving as a cavalry officer with considerable distinction in both the Boer War and in the First World War. Among his medals were the DSO, the Légion d'Honneur and the Croix de Guerre, and he was eventually appointed Aide-de-camp to King Albert of the Belgians. His three sisters, incidentally, were Maids of Honour to successive Queens Victoria, Alexandra and Elizabeth II. One of them was to marry Field-Marshal Earl Haig, while George himself married Barbara Fanning, an Edwardian beauty with aspirations to go on the stage.

This marriage was turbulent from the start. When they first set up house together, their quarrels were so violent that after exhausting every throwable object in the room, they would use the baby as a missile. That baby was my mother. A year and a half later, a second baby was born. This was my Uncle Tony. Then a couple of years later still, Barbara ran off with another gentleman, leading to an embittered divorce suit. Cruelty had only recently been introduced as legal grounds for divorce, and it was cited for the very first time in Barbara's cross-petition against George.

Nevertheless it was the father who retained custody, and Barbara's name was no longer to be mentioned within the household.

Not that this prevented Daphne from gleaning all the information she could about her disgraced mother – like the fact that she finally achieved her ambition by going on the stage – certainly not the profession for a lady of rank in that day and age.

But this wasn't all that Barbara achieved. Over the course of a long life she acquired five husbands in succession, and two additional children – with all but the final marriage being terminated by her sudden decision to bolt. Nancy Mitford is said to have been inspired by her example to create her own fictional character of 'the Bolter'. In any case there was a romantic side to such notoriety, and Daphne grew up craving to learn more about the absent mother whom no one was allowed to mention, while at the same time both hero-worshipping and yet being terrified by her excessively dominant father.

Daphne had far more contact throughout childhood with her two grandmothers who wholeheartedly detested each other after all the family mud-slinging engendered by the divorce. There was Louisa Alice Duff, the former Ambassadress, and there was 'Mouse' de Bathe, who first married Robert (or William Atmar) Fanning and then the wealthy Harry McCalmont. She was a notable traveller and socialite. But if she levelled the charge of insanity at the rival grandmother, she had much to excuse herself in her choice of Barbara's father, Robert (or William Atmar) Fanning, who was perhaps equally insane. In any case he was an alcoholic, with a vile temper.

One story about him tells how he brought two prostitutes back home with him, and then obliged them at pistol-point to undress and climb into bed with his wife, threatening to shoot the first lady to attempt an escape. And there they remained all night, although the tale doesn't furnish any enlightenment on how the situation progressed – apart from the fact that no one got shot. But Robert Fanning soon absconded from the scene ... setting a fine example, one might note, to his young daughter Barbara.

My grandfather George was more fortunate in his choice of a bride in his second marriage, which was to Nancy Lycett-Green, by whom he produced two more children, my Aunt Vanda and my Uncle Douglas. Nancy was a Master of Hounds and a spouse far better fitted to George's own temperament, in that she was good-natured and (on the surface) placidly pliable – while at the same time keeping him under firm control in that she held the purse-strings. To all appearances George may have dominated the family, but he must now have found himself financially restrained by the strong family ties of the Lycett-Green clan. The young Daphne was therefore given a comparatively stable upbringing, albeit as the daughter of a disgraced mother, and she was sent off to a variety of boarding-schools, from which she was invariably expelled.

When in 1926 my father Henry and my mother Daphne were intending to become officially engaged, the two families were by no means enthused by the prospect. Thomas, my paternal grandfather, wrote to George, my maternal grandfather, to say that Henry was too young to think of marrying and needed a very steady wife. To this Lord Vivian bombastically replied that he disapproved of Henry and thought he would be a most unsuitable match for his daughter, to whom he intended making this thoroughly clear.

That is as much of the exchange of opinions that has gone down on official record. But unofficially, the Thynnes were even more concerned about what they regarded as the bad Vivian blood. People didn't usually talk about suspect genes in those days, but it was pointed out quite accurately that a sizeable proportion of the Vivians and their collateral relations had spent considerable proportions of their lives hospitalised within asylums. Not that Henry's parents had any just cause to feel complacent about their own genes. Lady Maudant had, after all, ended her days in such a place. But their general feeling was that Daphne was flighty, like her mother, and might well bring some additional insanity into subsequent generations of a staid and respectable family.

Henry's parents felt that the wisest approach was to persuade him to spend a year in America, by which time they hoped that Daphne's hold over him would have been broken. But my mother had no intention of giving him up quite so easily. At this particular period in their lives, Daphne was dominant, in that she was six months older than my father, and knew the ropes – so to speak – whereas Henry had been over-protected as a child. We shouldn't forget that he was his parents' one remaining hope for an heir to Longleat, in direct line of descent from themselves.

So my mother persuaded my father to marry her in secret, just before setting sail for America, where he spent six months working on a Texan cattle-ranch. His parents then relented, writing to say that he could return – but the marriage remained a secret even after that. Since all parental opposition to such a wedding had now been withdrawn, the young marrieds felt it prudent to say nothing about the legal splicing that had already occurred. Instead, they displayed a commendable compliance with all that their parents suggested to them by way of playing the starring roles in the social big event of the London season: their second, and this time official, wedding. This was in 1927.

Daphne's viewpoint on her new family, as an outsider, changed on closer acquaintance. 'The silent Thynnes' had been the descriptive term in general circulation around London at that time – from which it might be inferred that the family was clannish, wrapped up in its own isolated perspective upon existence, and shy of attempting communication with any wider audience. But Daphne discovered how this reputation was in stark contrast to the atmosphere which prevailed when the Thynne clan was gathered at Longleat for the celebration of seasonal events like Christmas.

She records that it was then a round of vehement exchanges between established sparring partners, all and sundry participating in a general chorus of clichéd personal jokes, delivered as old chestnuts, in a cross between affection and malice, and giving rise to shrieks of laughter and outbursts of ritual singing.

My grandfather had never greatly admired my father's capacity for hard work. But the need now was for Henry to settle down, and Thomas was aware that his son's passion was for Longleat and its estate. So inasmuch that he himself had never relished the sheer banality of estate management, he now decided to place his son in charge of it. There were rapidly some misgivings, however, when Henry's enthusiasm prompted him to build a new piggery for the home farm, in a fashion which Thomas had been brought up to believe unnecessarily extravagant. Besides, the new buildings had been mistakenly sited: too far from the farm, and unprotected from the wind. And when the tenant farmer gave up breeding his pigs there, my father decided that he preferred the forestry to the agricultural side of the estate's industry. It was safer too, in that there was time enough to await the harvesting of his new plantations without any immediate economic assessment of what his managerial skills might be worth.

There had already been one other apparent failure in Henry's incipient career. At Queen Mary's insistence, he had been appointed to the Council to advise the Prince of Wales in his running of the Duchy of Cornwall. My father was to retain throughout his life a sincere admiration for Edward VIII, as he later became — both as a romantic and as someone eminently up front in the trend-setting social elite. But this esteem was never reciprocated, and the Thynne family felt some chagrin when the Prince requested that young Henry should send in his resignation.

The loss of that position meant little to him personally, since his interest in life was already focused upon the Longleat estate. As a young married couple he and his wife had befriended Russell Page, the newly fashionable landscape gardener, and it was largely at his inspiration that Henry now turned his thoughts to the possibility of beautifying Loncombe Drive, at the entrance to the park, with a blaze of colourful rhododendrons and azaleas, replacing the common varieties which were already growing there in profusion. It was a task they tackled piecemeal over the course of the next decade, with ultimate spectacular effect.

Henry was also concerned to upgrade the commercial potential of the Cheddar caves. Plans were now formulating in his head to build a complex of buildings, including a restaurant, on land at the opening of Gough's cave. The project was not to be completed until 1933, but the decisions were taken at this earlier time and focused on the augmentation of the scale of the whole enterprise at Cheddar.

There was also much else to occupy Henry's mind, for in deference to his father's ethos of public service, he agreed to stand for Parliament as the Conservative candidate for Frome. First, he had to spend a couple of years wooing the electorate, opening bazaars and the like. But he was finally elected to the House of Commons in 1931. It maintained the Tory-dominated National government in power, although with the former Labour premier Ramsey Macdonald still theoretically at the helm.

All of this electioneering took place while I was actually on the way, so to speak, awaiting the time of birth within my mother's womb. But I wasn't the first, or even the second, child born to Henry and Daphne.

Caroline, my elder sister, arrived in 1928, almost four years prior to myself. Henry's mother, Violet, died shortly prior to her birth, firmly predicting that she knew the child was going to be a son, because the sex (in her view) was determined as being the opposite of the dominant parent's. Henry was furious that she didn't live long enough to see that she was mistaken.

Then a year later came Timothy, my elder brother, but he survived for less than a year due to respiratory defects involving a collapsed lung. This then brings the story of my ancestral background to the very threshold of my own birth – from which point, I shall resume the tale in the next chapter.

However, let me first say a few words in summary of the general picture that I have described at such length over this and the previous four chapters.

There was never a question of my entering upon life's stage as an independent entity, my parents concerned to nourish any divergent degree of individualism that might emerge. I was conceived for their purpose of furnishing an heir to Longleat, and all individualism was expected to remain subordinate to that end. Traditions and expectations had to be learnt from the very start, but also the distinction between Thynne and Vivian family traditions and expectations. For there was a potential schism involved – particularly if we assess these concerns through the eyes of the two people who had married to become my parents.

The Thynnes, as my father viewed them, were a Saxon family of down-to-earth unpretentious respectability, with no fuss and nonsense about intellect or art, but a tradition to uphold as pillars of the establishment within the West Country at large. They had always been regarded as a family of outstanding significance within that arena, but they had never quite managed to produce any giant upon the national scene. Respected, but mediocre, could have been an outsider's verdict.

The Vivians, on the other hand, as my mother viewed them, were a Celtic family of military and monarchist traditions, with a flair for adventure and daring. They were also less Philistine – more concerned about literature and art.

But my father and mother were united in feeling that the First World War had swept aside the rigid conventions of the Victorian and Edwardian eras, and that they themselves were representative of the new breed of young people, eager to profit from the general release from social restraints. All this combined with a fundamental conventionality concerning upper-class social *mores*. They were rebels against all outdated stuffiness, and yet they believed quite firmly in their own aristocratic elitism.

It was from origins such as these that my own sense of identity, and my own sense of revolt, were gradually to coalesce. I don't suppose it ever occurred to my parents, for a single second, that they themselves had initiated a revolt against the established traditions which, as I see it, was to become my own role in its ultimate clarification and fulfilment.

# PART TWO

# CHILDHOOD

❊

# Chapter 7

## Parents: Discovering my initial relationships

My parents were on holiday in Venice at the time I was probably conceived. They were the guests of Laura Corrigan, the American hostess who, despite her suspect origins (of being a sometime waitress, managing to marry an elderly millionaire who promptly expired from a heart attack) and despite the fact that New York society had turned their backs on her, was currently making quite some splash upon the European social scene. My father and mother were amongst those of *la jeunesse dorée* who had been enticed to her parties with extravagant gifts of jewellery concealed within the napkins at each table-setting. In fact, they were particular favourites of hers, and for the summer of 1931 they had been invited to stay with her at the Palazzo Mocenigo in Venice, where Byron had formerly lived for a short while. I have often wondered if it was in Byron's bed that I was actually conceived.

Apparently I was a nuisance during the final month of pregnancy, in that I did not readily submit to birth. I was late, and Daphne found it tedious to be constantly parading her hippopotamus-like shape at social gatherings upon the London scene. But finally, at about 19.00 hours on 6 May 1932, in 95 Seymour Place, London W1, assisted by a midwife known universally as Nanny B, my mother gave me birth – to the great rejoicing of the Thynne family (apart, I dare say, from the distant Thynne cousins who were thus removed yet one step further from the line of succession to Longleat). To Henry my father, and to Thomas my grandfather, and to all the kith and kin of my father's three sisters, it was indeed splendid news that there was finally, or rather, once again, a direct heir within the main branch of the family.

So the feeling of being much wanted, in the sense that I was in some way the fulfilment of a parental ambition, was fed to me within my mother's milk. It gave me an idea of self-importance, I suppose – and in those days it produced a direct bonding between Daphne and myself. It was a warmth of special regard that seemed to emanate from her.

> Orbiting **thoughtl**ess, I **caught** my **clasp** on a **comet**'s
> bri**d**al **train**, to be **drawn** in**side** it, and **lift**ed,
> as **gifts one** to the **oth**er, **lov**ers at **birth**,
> **worth more** than **any** in**fin**ite **fig**ure.
> **Big-bos**omed to my **dripp**ing **lips**, you **slipped** me
> a **safe** em**brace, bountiful** in **beautiful grace**
> and **favour**. I **sa**voured **all** with **small greed**y
> **gulps**, feel**ing sure** how **batt**les are **won**.
> The **sun kissed blissfully** the **win**dow **net**ting,
> **lett**ing a **little** of the **mor**ning **light seep**
> **sweet**ly in a **white mist** to the **plush carp**et,
> **lush**ly **wrapp**ing our **happy feet** on the **floor**.
> The toils of life I now could undertake,
> no matter how this planet Earth might quake.

My feeling towards Henry were always more reserved. When he sold the house in Seymour Place, he bought one in Tite Street, Chelsea. It was to be the family's town house over the period that he was a Conservative Member of Parliament, which was only until the election of 1935, although it was not finally sold until 1938.

We were in the dining-room at Tite Street, Henry standing, Daphne seated, and myself on the floor. Dad's general approach towards me was often to adopt a teasing tone, which I frequently misread. He demanded: 'Which of us do you like the better? Mummy or Daddy? Come on – you can tell us. We won't be angry.' So I told him it was Mummy – and promptly felt uncertain and nervous of myself to perceive his reaction, which was one of evident displeasure. In fact, he left the room. Whereupon Mum went to great pains to explain to me that what I ought to have answered was that I loved the two of them equally, which was such an evident falsehood that I couldn't understand why she wanted me to say such things. Yet even as she said so, I perceived with an inner comprehension from her coyly smiling expression that she was really delighted by what I had said, and was merely reproving me out of what eventually came to be identified as marital loyalty.

The next essential image of my relationship with Henry came a little while later, when I was four. We had moved to Sturford Mead in Corsley, near Longleat, which was a delightful Georgian manor house with a spacious garden including a large pond, plus outbuildings. This was now our principal place of residence, and we were in the dining-room. My father was smoking and in a convivial mood. Holding out his hand towards me, he asked: 'Would you like to see smoke come out of my ears? Well, give me your hand, and watch them very closely while I concentrate upon what I'm doing.' He was seated, so his head was only slightly higher than my own, and I gazed as bidden with all the interest that his proposition deserved. But while I gazed, he moved his other hand which held the cigarette, to touch (oh so lightly) the back of the small hand I had innocently entrusted to him.

I can still fiercely remember the fury that I felt.

'That was an imp's trick!' I shouted, for an imp was then the vilest form of abuse that I could muster. But Henry was roaring with laughter, and there was nobody sympathetic to my plight. I felt indignation, and resented that it should be dismissed as an inability, on my side, to perceive somehow that it was supposed to be funny.

> **Did** it **please** you to **wit**ness the **sud**den **switch**
> from **rich** ex**pec**tant **trust** to a **twitch** of **pain**,
> sa**dist**ically **gain**ing **tit**illation for your **mad**
> **man**ia in **see**ing your **titch** of a **son** so **cross**?
> **Was** it for a **wag's gig**gle, like **watch**ing a **car**pet
> **sharp**ly **tugged**, to **top**ple the **un**suspecting
> **pomp**ous **child**, **open**ing his **in**nocent **eyes**
> to a **wis**er, **untrust**ing **slip**pery **world**?
> Or **third**ly, **was** it your **exhibi**tionist **side**,
> **snide**ly **steal**ing the **spot**-lit **circle** with a **rot**ten
> **trick**, **slick**ly **im**itating a **con**juror's
> **won**drous **ways** in **mag**ic? – with **what** a **wand**!
>     In treachery, I glimpsed you to the heart
>     and knew, somewhere within, we stood apart.

# Chapter 8

## Siblings: Finding my niche in the family

Caroline was there from the start. She was my constant companion, in those early days. Older than myself by three and three-quarter years, she knew the ropes and was protective of my interests with regard to life outside the walls of our nursery sanctuary. She knew (and probably deemed it unfair) that I was something unique within the family – the treasured heir. But she accepted her guardianship role with a possessiveness that was quite fierce. Others might display a rather special concern about my welfare, but there was never any challenge from me to her personal dominance. I belonged to her, and could be trained to suit her ways.

Caroline's particular method of controlling me was by sensory deprivation, by which I mean that she would suddenly refuse to communicate with me until I had bent my will to hers. I invariably felt miserable while this mode of persuasion was being applied, and my one concern was to reopen the full bonding of her grace and favour. A sense of pride in my own human rights was quite evidently lacking.

I loved Caroline, and whatever she told me I believed. Mummy and Nanny would read us fairy stories, and Caroline confided to me that she herself was a fairy. If I had been so bold as to disobey her, which I seldom did, she would have turned me into a toad. But in my obedience to her, I was rewarded with many a special treat. I sinned once, however.

This was at a party in London, when I informed another boy who was neglecting to show my sister the reverence she deserved, that she was a fairy, so he'd better watch out. His ribald laughter took me by surprise and offended me, and I noted how Caroline looked put out. What disappointed me was that she refrained from turning him into a toad. She was at pains to impress on me, later, that this being-a-fairy business was secret between ourselves. I must not divulge it to others. But I heard rather less about her magic powers after that.

If Caroline told me to run errands, I would run them. I was hers to command, and pleased that this should be so. The birth of a younger brother did nothing to alter any of that. I have no distinct memory of Christopher arriving upon the scene, almost two years later than myself. Nobody (apart from Nanny) treated him as a significant addition to the family, and he was generally left behind in her care when Caroline and I accompanied our parents to whatever might be going on. My first significant memory of Christopher was when our family doctor enquired what I thought of my little brother.

I said: 'He wets his bed.'

Christopher's initial statement of identity was as the naughty one within the family. Caroline and I were shocked at the way he beamed with pleasure when standing up in his cot, advertising the fact that, once again, he had performed this trick. He got smacked for it on successive occasions – until Dr Graham-Campbell suggested, gently, that this might be the motivation which prompted the bed-wetting. So thenceforward he was punished by Nanny's omission to smack him.

It was still by naughtiness that he best gained the family attention, however. He was only three when my father took us all to the Norfolk Broads for a holiday on board a boat called *The Wherry*. Christopher continually managed to escape from the cabin where he had been confined as a punishment, by climbing out of a port-hole. Henry tried to break this habit by beating him (lightly enough, I dare say) with the top section of a fishing rod. Later, I was to hear my father say that he had been greatly impressed by the little boy's cheerfulness under such treatment – the one responding to the other, perhaps, in what was the initiation of a special relationship. The exact working of this was something that I never did comprehend.

Christopher was exceptionally slow in learning how to speak. To such an extent that Henry was concerned at one point to discover if it might be necessary to have an operation performed upon his tongue, which gave the impression of being too large for his mouth. He was unable to pronounce his own name, which came out sounding something like 'Pip – Pip – '.

Hence it was Pip-Pip that we called him, and soon afterwards, just Pip. Caroline's name became abbreviated to Cal, incidentally, and my own to Al – until the time we went to school, that is to say.

My own viewpoint upon Pip was that he was a nuisance. Daddy had rules about not leaving our toys downstairs in the drawing-room. If we did so, they would be confiscated and given away to the local orphanage. And once rules had been made, they had to be strictly applied – in the interests of discipline and the development of obedience.

It is probable that I possessed many more toys than Christopher, but I seldom took this into account when he left my toys down in the drawing-room, with the result that they were confiscated. It was no good hoping that my father might bend the rules under such circumstances. Rules were rules, and they had to be applied.

I had a new game called Helter-Skelter, involving marbles rolled down a spiral chute, to score points in accordance with the hole they entered upon the final slope. I'd only just been given it, so I was particularly upset when Pip left this downstairs. The rule couldn't be broken, but I obtained Henry's permission to exchange the item that was to be confiscated for something else, of lesser personal value.

I had a large menagerie of cuddly toy animals, each with a distinct personality of its own, and I concluded that one of these must be sacrificed. Two of them were pigs, so perhaps one might be regarded as superfluous. Tommy Pig had been with me for a long time, and it was because he had lost most of his stuffing that I had recently been presented by my parents with Percy Pig, who was far classier and probably came from Harrods. But I hadn't yet developed a feeling of relationship with him, so it had to be he – a decision that nonetheless cost me many tears.

The expression on my mother's face was even more woebegone than my own, however, when I went to make the exchange. They had chosen Percy Pig for me with some care, and at no little expense – to wean me of my adoration for Tommy Pig. And here I was trading him in for a rubbishy game of marbles, which had cost a few shillings at the most. Rules were rules, though, and they had to be strictly applied. So it was goodbye to Percy.

When I did play with Pip, it was not exactly as equals. I got into trouble on one occasion because a gardener at Sturford Mead reported to Nanny that I was dragging the poor little mite around the garden with a rope around his neck. He made it sound as if I'd been intending to string him up, and that his life had only been saved by intervention in the nick of time. But it was a simple case of grown-ups getting things wrong. We'd been playing at cowboys – and Pip was my steer.

On another occasion we were playing robbers, and we had sticks as swords. It was old Mrs Garrett's misfortune to come walking down the lane from Corsley at this juncture. We jumped her from the bushes, and threatened to cut off her head with our swords. Nanny got to hear of this, and we were sent down to apologise to Mrs Garrett for our assault. I always assumed that it had been the old lady herself who must have lodged a complaint. But I was to learn many years later, from Nanny, that it was Cal who had spotted what we were up to, and reported us. I believe that Caroline played this sort of role more often than we suspected at the time. She liked to be in control of events, and this robbers game was not of her own making.

I was five and a half when my youngest brother, Valentine, was born. I remember his arrival, and we all got excited about it at the time. But it wasn't as if Cal and I were going to permit him to play a significant part in our lives. He was Nanny's favourite, of course. She always treasured the youngest addition to the family, extending to him the special cloak of her protection – spoiling him, as we saw it. And it could be that he had some need of this, if the truth be told.

There is one shameful story which had best be recounted. Valentine (or Baba, as he came to be known until his schooldays) was such an inanimate creature, and it was almost in a spirit of scientific curiosity that Pip and I put nettles at the foot of his pram – just to see if his feet were truly sensitive. They were, of course, and he started howling with pain, without displaying an awareness of who might be inflicting it upon him. At that moment Nanny fortuitously arrived upon the scene, kicking up one hell of a fuss. I was the culprit, of course. Pip had only been watching what I did. And Nanny flounced off declaring that she was going to tell Mummy about what I'd been up to.

I followed her at a distance, and when I looked in at the drawing-room window, I espied that she was deep in a serious conversation with Daphne. Entering by the bay window, I said: 'I'm sorry, Mummy. I'm sorry.' It then became apparent that Nanny had in fact refrained from betraying me, so that I was now obliged to come out with my own confession – which may have been the circumstance that saved me from the punishment I merited.

In the summer of 1938, the whole family was holidaying at Piraillan, near Arcachon and Bordeaux in France. Henry had rented a house right down on the beach, and in different ways our respective personalities became noticeable. Baba for his part was delighting the family with little cabaret performances. When held just above the surface of the sea, he did 'splashy-splashies' with his feet, or 'smelly-smellies' with a crinkled nose when presented with a flower.

Pip's persona had taken a more erotic turn. Cal told me how she had seen him taking down his bathing pants to display his bottom to a young French girl who dwelt in one of the neighbouring houses. I had made no progress, personally, in breaking the language barrier between myself and these French girls, and Christopher's evident success in this more direct approach struck me as shocking. Cal too had seemed to be shocked when telling me what he had done. So I fell into the trap of giving vent to my moral indignation when passing on the story to my parents. Cal betrayed me, however, by switching tone and telling them that I too had done precisely the same thing. I denied this indignantly.

'I didn't!'

'You did.'

'I didn't.'

'You did.'

And inasmuch that she was older than me, I received the uncomfortable impression that her word was being taken in preference to my own. This was an initial insight into my sister's highly flexible concept of truth.

The distinction between Caroline's and my own attitude in other matters came vividly to the forefront of attention when the French cook in our house at Piraillan had a live cockerel to slaughter for our lunch. She imagined that this would be a spectacle that would both interest and educate us, so she brought out the bird into the garden where we were playing, and stuck a carving knife down its throat so that an artery was severed, and the blood began to flow. I regret to say that my own interest was aroused. But Cal was of gentler spirit, displaying her disgust in no uncertain fashion, and when it came to her refusal to partake of flesh from the cockerel we had seen slaughtered, she had me wrong-footed, torn between the demands of my hunger and my fraternal desire to display ideological solidarity. Greed won the day, and I ate my share of the bird – while Cal missed out on lunch altogether.

The Munich crisis interrupted this holiday down in Piraillan, and we drove north in a frantic hurry to get back on the right side of the Channel. Tempers frayed quickly under such conditions, and when Pip and I went on imitating the noise and the manoeuvres of circling fighter planes from our seats in the back of the car after one warning, Henry's patience with us snapped. Slamming on the brakes, he bade me step outside with him, whereupon I was spanked. Cal reported to me later how Pip was giggling away happily at the sight of all this. But then my father summoned him to a similar fate, and his tune rapidly changed.

'No, please, Daddy! No, please!'

Henry was later to recount how he had no heart to spank the little boy too fiercely after that.

Cal was in fact beginning to distance herself from me over the latter part of this period. The age-gap of nearly four years was in fact quite a hurdle to surmount. So long as I was prepared to be her personal servant, all had been well. Nor do I feel that she had greatly abused her status over me. It was the fact that she never really did make too heavy demands, relying more on the nuance of the elder-sister relationship to get what she wanted from me, which made my affection for her so durable. But I was beginning to find that there was more I could do with Pip than with her, and I never managed to feel comfortable when she was in the presence of her particular local girl-friend, who was Diana Phipps from Chalcot House. It was girls' talk the whole time between the two of them, even in my presence, and my efforts to participate in such conversations merely led to some snide suggestions from Diana that I was probably a girlish sort of boy. In some ways my identity felt more secure when in the company of my brothers.

I can also remember that while I was seven years old, Cal informed me (what she had no doubt been hearing from others) that I was 'passing through an awkward age.' I found this to be a description which, once applied, was never to be retracted. By now, however, I find that I can live with it.

# Chapter 9

## Hierarchy:
## Learning my status

One of my very earliest memories can be dated precisely to my third birth-day. I was standing up in the back of an open car, waving a small Union Jack in acknowledgement to the joyous acclamation of a London crowd. Daddy was telling me that they were gathered there because it was my special day to celebrate. Only later was it admitted that there had been additional cause for the crowd's festivity in that 6 May 1935 happened to be the date of King George V's Silver Jubilee. Even then I regarded it as evidence that there must be a special relationship between the two of us. I had my picture of him hanging up in the nursery, and taking my cue from the national anthem, I referred to him always as 'My Gracious King'.

My parents had always been steeped in an aristocratic elitism, such as Daphne's friend Nancy Mitford was to portray more openly in literary form. There were upper-class ways of both doing and saying whatever needed to be done or said, and conversely, there were non-U ways for people to brand themselves in such judgement as coming from an inferior sort of background.

In Nancy's books there is a salutary undercurrent of mirth beneath the whole snobbish business. But with my parents, such values were ingrained to the extent of their being taken very seriously. And we children had to learn such pitfalls in either behaviour or language, in much the same way as in Divinity class at school we had to learn the Ten Commandments.

To mention some trivial examples, it was a sin to refer to the drawing-

room by any other name – such as the lounge, or parlour. We never went
to the toilet. It was to the lavatory, or loo. Our eating utensils must be held
in the correct manner, with their handles in the centre of the palm, and
with our index fingers extended down the spine of each instrument. It was
inadmissible to put fish knives on the dining-table, to carry a comb, or to
pronounce the letter L in the word 'golf'. Joining in a chorus of 'Cheers!'
when toasting was to stick in my throat for many years to come. Instead of
that, we had to say 'Your good health!' We never failed to notice, and to
comment upon it later, if people who had come to tea, poured their milk
in first, and then the tea. This branded them as 'MIF', in abbreviation of
the phrase. And the ultimate shibboleth was in the use of the word
'Pardon?', which had to be avoided at all costs, unless it were integrated
within some longer phrase like 'I beg your pardon.' 'What?' or 'Sorry?'
were the more acceptable upper-class equivalents.

Avoidance of their gentle ridicule was the most usual incentive for
learning, but Henry also indulged in the tactics of the short, sharp shock.
The proclaimed faults in my table manners were rapidly eliminated after I
had experienced one of his lightning raps from the bowl of a desert spoon
upon my funny-bone to deter me from ever again placing my elbows on
the table.

We were brought up to regard ourselves as superior sort of people,
although it was never spelt out precisely what that superiority entailed.
There was some vague idea about us all having 'class', as if it must be something perceptible, and as if the colour of our blood was literally blue. But
we were made aware that this was a delicate subject that we couldn't discuss with others – not even with Nanny, for example – because they didn't
have 'class', so they wouldn't understand what we were talking about, and
might even be offended if they tried. There was also an awareness that we
might be accused of snobbishness if some of the things said in private
between ourselves were to be overheard by others.

The importance of who I was, and of what I was going to become, was
never too far from my mind. When I was seven, a couple of our footmen
put that very question to me – perhaps for the reason that they knew damn
well I wasn't going to reply that I wanted to be an engine-driver, a soldier,
or even a prime minister. I informed them, as indeed I had been told, that
I was going to be the Marquess of Bath.

During those years of early childhood, before the war, our status as
members of the family was held clearly in focus by all of our domestic staff.
We were addressed as Master Alexander or Miss Caroline, never by the first

name on its own. Nanny alone was permitted such intimate address, and she inferred from this that she stood somewhere in status between the family and the domestic staff – a point which she never allowed those under her to forget.

That relations between Nanny and the domestic staff could be frictional is perhaps best illustrated by the anecdote frequently related to us over subsequent years of how a particular cook, who didn't remain with us for very long, objected to the criticisms that were relayed down to the kitchen by the footman who came to collect the dirty dishes, to the effect that the meat course on the nursery menu had been overcooked. Next day, when the cover was removed from the plate, the sight of a raw skinned rabbit greeted our eyes. Anyway, that was the fashion in which Nanny described it. And by her account, after the scene which followed, attendants from the nearest lunatic asylum were called to cart off this cook to where she belonged.

But there were clear limits to Nanny's authority, as it rapidly became evident to me that authority stemmed from Daddy. People jumped to obey what he dictated, and I knew that Mummy wouldn't actually contradict what he decreed. Nanny's authority didn't carry any manner of equivalent weight.

This was proven to me at an early age, when I was complaining to her about having to go downstairs for Sunday lunch, which had recently been established as a regular event, but which I was anxious to avoid because luncheons downstairs were far more disciplined than our meals upstairs in the nursery. So I was seated there at the top of the front stairs, snivelling my resentment, in the hopes that Nanny would take me back under her protective wing.

She was preening herself, no doubt, in such evident display of my preference for her company, and she was murmuring words of consolation in my ear about soon having her back again, or whatever. Then came Henry's trumpeting bellow from his study downstairs, ordering Nanny's retreat to the nursery, which was promptly obeyed. My whining also ceased instantly at his command, and I was never heard to make a fuss about going downstairs to lunch after that. We all understood that Daddy's authority was paramount within the household.

When it came to the subject of our grandparents, whether at Longleat or at Glynn (the house in Cornwall where Grandpa Vivian dwelt), we understood that the authority of each upon his own territory was to be regarded as supreme. Each was a considerable personality in his own right

– Thomas in his reverenced dignity and lofty reserve, and George in his peppery individualism and coercive bombast. I was aware how each was to be respected, and I revered them ... without managing to feel that I ever made any special impression upon their affections.

The battle for status came to a head at gatherings of the Thynne clan at Longleat over Christmas. Thomas allotted each family its own special nursery, Henry (his son and heir) having what was traditionally the nursery, on the second floor of the North Wing of the house. Kathleen and Mary, both of them elder sisters with families of their own, had to make do with spare nurseries up on the top floor.

Kathleen had married Oliver Stanley, heir presumptive of Lord Stanley of Alderley, and her brood consisted of four sons, all of them older than myself. Nanny Harrod was in charge of them, and was senior in age and experience to Nanny Marks. Moreover, she had the support of Nanny Bolton, who looked after Mary's two boys and a girl: Mary had married John Lord Numburnholm, and her Wilson children were of approximately the same age as Henry's own. But Nanny Harrod put forward the case that nurseries should have been allotted in accordance with the order in which Lord Bath's children had been born, which would have dropped our brood to the bottom of the list – something that would have put Nanny Marks firmly in her place, as her two rivals would have liked to think. But she certainly wasn't going to stand for that, and the case was taken to my grandfather, who was content to abide by tradition and his former judgement, insisting that the allotted nurseries remain as he had ordained.

The snobbery of the upbringing was rammed home to us not only in the acquired values of Nanny Marks but also by Miss Vigers, who became our governess. Each of them was *sine nobilitas*, of course, but they had the opportunity often enough to listen in on the way our parents talked about life in the company of their own family, and Miss Vigers in any case had known previous such experience in that, amongst others, she had taught George and Gerald Lascelles, the children of the Princess Royal. Many years later, when comparing family memories about Miss Vigers with the former Countess of Harewood, who had been married to George, I learnt how the Lascelles boys had observed that without apparently being aware of what she was doing she would bob up and down in curtsies whenever she had the Princess Royal speaking to her on the phone. But in any case, she regarded herself as a real specialist in aristocratic ways.

Not that Nanny Marks was ever going to let it be said that she knew less on the subject than Miss Vigers, for the two spinsters (the former middle-aged and the latter elderly) detested each other to the core.

There had been a power struggle when Miss Vigers had first arrived, which was in 1938. She wasn't our first governess, but she was the only one to take up the thorny question of whether governess or nanny had precedence within the family hierarchy. Her subtle scheme was to persuade my mother that she could save herself a lot of bother by entrusting the house accountancy to herself – which just incidentally included the task of paying the servants. Daphne unwisely agreed to the suggestion. But when Nanny learnt that she was now expected to queue up with the servants every Saturday to receive her wages from the hand of Miss Vigers, she went on strike. She reminded everyone that she was employed by Lady Weymouth, and not by Miss Vigers. So Daphne felt obliged to acknowledge that Nanny was not to be treated as one of the servants, and henceforward was paid separately, much to the governess' chagrin.

The power struggle thereafter was more a question of who had the right to exercise influence over us children. Caroline and myself had separate bedrooms downstairs, adjacent to that of Miss Vigers, while Christopher and Valentine remained upstairs in the nursery, still under the care and protection of Nanny. It was only during the holidays that all four children were recombined, and even this led to problems on occasions.

For example, there was the day when Miss Vigers returned from her holiday to find that one pair of Caroline's pink knickers could not be accounted for. She made a special point of keeping lists of everything, so she took the appropriate list up to the nursery, demanding an explanation. But Nanny was in no mood to be cross-examined on the subject, so held the door firmly closed in her face – something that the governess found most offensive.

There followed a farcical scene in which they both shouted at one another through the closed door, Miss Vigers demanding instant admission, while Nanny confined herself to disclaiming any knowledge of the missing pair of pink knickers. After persistent accusation, however, she changed her story, and declared that she had eaten them. Not that this did anything to soften Miss Vigers' insistence that the door be opened so that she could explore the nursery wardrobe for herself. And she was now pushing vigorously against the door, in the knowledge that her superior weight must surely win the day against her far lighter opponent.

At this juncture, however, Nanny chose to step aside while pulling the door open, saying: 'Then come in, Miss Vigers!' – which she did, of course falling flat on her face. This story was related to us subsequently, on numerous occasions, by the triumphant nurse.

The idea of a cultural divide between schoolroom and nursery was promoted by Miss Vigers, rather than by Nanny. In the eyes of the governess, time was on her side. Children went through a natural progression in their process of education, and there was a point when nurses became expendable. If she were to bide her time, she anticipated that Nanny would soon be retired.

But she wasn't content to bide her time. She wanted Nanny to know that she was on the slippery slope to enforced retirement.

I can remember one fierce exchange between the two of them, when meeting on the stairs, Nanny clutching Baba to her breast as if the devil incarnate intended to snatch him away from her. And Miss Vigers was saying sarcastically: 'Yes, Nanny, I'll have that one too. He'll grow up in due course, and then he'll be mine!'

We didn't really like Miss Vigers. It was Cal who initiated our Secret Club, whose only real purpose was as a forum where our identity (uncontrolled by Miss Vigers) could be effectively discussed. Our meetings were held within the sheltering seclusion of a yew tree, down in the garden near the garage. We had recently been given a typewriter by Mrs Corrigan, and Cal put it to instant use in drawing up the list of rules of conduct and admissibility, ending up with the minutes of our first meeting.

Unhappily, she left these on a table, where they came to Miss Vigers' attention. We regarded it as typical of this authoritarian old cow that she should promptly read them – despite the word 'SECRET' written in capital letters and underlined. And the penalty she imposed upon Cal for initiating such a spirit of revolt was to make her sit down and copy it all out again, with all of her numerous spelling mistakes corrected.

We disliked Miss Vigers because she was old, ugly and fierce. Nanny might cluck like a hen, but she was kindly and one hundred per cent loyal to the entire family. We made jokes about the way the two of them were perpetually trying to run each other down, but we never hoped that Miss Vigers would achieve ultimate victory. At this stage, however, it rather looked as if she might.

Nanny's slant of control over us was to assume a pose of martyrdom, simulating the imminent advent of a nervous breakdown which never in fact arrived. Or perhaps it really did. Anyway, by her account, the time came when she awoke one morning and found she simply hadn't the energy to move. So Dr Graham-Campbell prescribed for her a long holiday, during the course of which her place was taken by a disagreeable old harridan who shall remain nameless. Naturally, Miss Vigers was full of her praises, bringing it to Lady Weymouth's attention wherever possible just how much better discipline her children were receiving from hands such as these, in comparison with those of Nanny Marks. Word somehow (and I know not from what quarter) reached Nanny that her job was on the line, and she abandoned her holiday forthwith – just in time to accompany us on that family holiday to Piraillan.

I suppose I was Miss Vigers' favourite. The fact that I was the future Marquess was sufficient to ensure that status, no matter what kind of personality I might display. But she bestowed upon Caroline and myself a feeling that we were the intelligentsia of the family, far superior in quality to either Pip or Baba.

When Christopher came to join us in the schoolroom, for some initial tuition on how to read and write, he only managed to infuriate Miss Vigers by watching her lips and endeavouring to guess the words he was supposed to be reading. And she insisted that he simply wasn't trying when he wrote down 'nymcut' as his best effort to spell the word 'country'. It never occurred to Miss Vigers that what he had in fact done was virtually to switch the syllables around, which could well be evidence that such scholastic ineptitude, effectively blighting his school career, possibly stemmed from a dyslexia that was never diagnosed as such. Whacking him across the knuckles with a ruler proved insufficient as a method of igniting his interest in education.

It was Miss Vigers who spelt out to us the snobbery that was implicit within our parents' attitudes. I learnt how the local dialect, as spoken by Tom Renyard, the gamekeeper my father had appointed to instruct me in rabbiting and shooting, was indicative of low breeding, and therefore a subject for private jokes. While friendly with his nephew, I was encouraged to preserve my distance from him. Much was made of the fact that he would not be going to the same kind of school as myself. As with members of the domestic staff, I knew that I should not confide my inner thoughts to him.

What I had in fact been initiated into was a system of hierarchy. The royal family was at the top, but my father wasn't all that far below. Where the Prime Minister might find his allotted place would depend more upon his breeding than upon his political eminence – and neither Mr Ramsey Macdonald, nor Mr Stanley Baldwin were at all well-bred. My father was most certainly to be regarded as supreme within the family environment, and my mother (now that she had entered the Thynne fold) would not have seen fit to dispute that she only came second. Henry had by now, in some way, replaced George Lord Vivian as the necessary dominant male within Daphne's life. And below her came her children, in the order of their birth.

During this my childhood, I was brought up to defer to the wishes of Caroline. One deferred to her for two reasons, because she was elder, and because she was female. All females were ushered through doors before myself, and they served themselves first at table. But it went deeper than this, in that Cal's preferences on any subject were demanded before my own. And I accepted all this without demur, because my own preferences had priority over those of Christopher or Valentine. Poor little Baba, if the truth be told, was supposed to defer to everybody, and would have had a wretched time if his interests hadn't been so stalwartly protected by Nanny.

# Chapter 10

## Activities:
## The established way to enjoy myself

We didn't see very much of our parents within a normal day's schedule. We'd go up to Daphne's bedroom to kiss her good morning, and perhaps stay with her while she finished her breakfast in bed, and took her morning bath. Henry was more usually up and away by that time, preferring to eat in the dining-room. And that might well be the last we saw of either of them until we were washed and brushed up, ready for the brief evening session downstairs in the drawing-room. The rest of the day was spent either in the garden or in the nursery upstairs. We saw a great deal more of Nanny than we did of either of my parents.

The Christmas season always sticks in my mind as being something very different, partly because we all moved into Longleat, and partly because there were so many other children (in the form of cousins) with whom to mingle. It was a fortifying experience to learn that we were all part of an integrated clan, concerned about each other's welfare. And there were ritual games of an evening, first and foremost amongst which for anyone still youthful enough to caper and cavort was Cocky-Olly – or Kick The Pot Out, as it was sometimes called elsewhere.

This entailed the person who was Cocky-Olly making sorties from a base territory, invariably sited half-way up the front stairs. By pronouncing the name of any individual, on sighting, they were captured, and upon the touch of anyone who remained uncaptured – so long as the touch was delivered within the home base – they were instantly released. And Henry was the adult by far the most preferred who ever volunteered to fulfil that role. This was because he knew how to combine the right degree of growling fierceness in pursuing us fleeing children, with the lenience of permitting us to get rescued once we had been garnered in his home den. His popularity as an uncle made me feel really proud of him actually being my father.

The excitement in the game also involved that question of hiding ourselves in dark corners and cachettes within Longleat's multiple galleries and corridors. The very idea of straying too far from the touch of our human kind evoked a sense of unease, or even terror, that we might encounter one of the ghosts whom we knew with conviction to populate this building. There were all those tales of the Grey Lady searching for her lost lover; or of the footman who died when falling down that spiral staircase. (The two stories were separate in my mind over that period.) And there were other fancies too, of a gory nature, relating to the monks from the original Longlete Priory. Even some inanimate objects like the two ebony statues of negro figures (to support flower arrangements) struck fear into our hearts whenever it was necessary to pass them, unaccompanied, on our way upstairs to our respective nurseries.

Some of the fun and games engendered seasonally at Longleat were for the wider audience of those who worked upon our estate. They often included amateur theatricals, performed by the assembled clan in the village hall at Horningsham. On my first such appearance, at two and a half, I can remember being dressed up in a clownish attire and required to follow my elder cousin, Richard Stanley, in simulating performing animals and coming down a slide at a crack of the ringmaster's (Henry's) whip. A year later I even had a speaking part. I was dressed in my pink pig-patterned pyjamas, with a top hat and soot on my face. I rushed out on stage waving a small handbrush, exclaiming: 'I'm getting on like a house on fire!' There was much applause, which I was given to understand that I had merited.

There were activities of a sort more typical within our social strand, to which I was introduced at the age of seven. When Henry had been a boy, and prior to being recognised as the heir to Longleat, he'd been impassioned by the outdoor life to which he was introduced by Dick Futcher, the gamekeeper to whose care and tutelage he had been entrusted by Thomas. Not that the introduction went without regrets, as Aunt Kathleen was to inform me. She told me there was something in Henry which always managed to shock Thomas.

'It was kill, kill, kill, the whole time. Your grandfather was such a gentle person. He could never understand how anybody could be so anxious to kill everything.'

My father was to tell me later that he always felt more at home with the Futchers' simple life than he did under the strict formality of the Longleat household. He regarded himself as a country boy at heart, which he held in sharp contrast to Daphne's social inclinations and general town culture. By introducing me to Tom Renyard, he imagined that he was pointing my footsteps in the same direction as his own – even if it wasn't to work out like that.

I had a liking and respect for Tom. He was uneducated, but greatly concerned about education – even a poor man's philosopher, in a small way. He was often encouraging me to compete with him in spelling-bees and the like. But my spelling was atrocious at that age, and I think somewhere the idea was understood that it would be inappropriate for me to compete, and get defeated by Tom. So we never really got together on an intellectual plane. And I think there were occasions when he was offended by reports from Mrs Sims, in the kitchen, on how we all made jokes about his Wessex accent. Mrs Sims was always a troublemaker (and I'll be saying more on that subject in due course).

During these years before I was packed off to boarding-school, however, most of my activities involved Tom's participation – whether in rabbiting, ratting, beating for the shooting parties, fishing, bicycling, or merely in catching butterflies. The latter sport was something that I introduced him to, rather than the other way around. I had been handed down the essentials for butterfly-collecting by my cousin Tom Stanley, who was Caroline's contemporary. It surprised many that Tom Renyard took to the sport with such enthusiasm. But he may have had the feeling that I wasn't really catching on to the blood-lust sports, to which it had been intended that I should be introduced, so he moved a little in my direction by way of compensation. I have visions of him with cloth cap and haversack, bounding over clumps of bracken in pursuit of fritillaries, butterfly net held aloft, and with the cyanide bottle extended in the other hand. It was similar to the sight of a dog bounding to retain vision of a rabbit in corn stubble.

I developed an interest, although not a passion, for natural history and animal life as a result of my days in the woods with Tom. I learnt something about birds, and the appeal of young nestlings, waiting open-beaked for the anticipated gift of worms. After seeing my first grass-snake, I spent hours in that vicinity, making noises on a toy piano-accordion which I had been given, supposing that this music would charm the reptile a second time from its lair.

But we did also do those other things. I was taught to overcome my squeamishness about lifting a blood-soaked rabbit from the ferret's clamped jaws, and breaking its neck with a deft downward wrench, before disembowelling it, and then stringing its legs crossed together so that the total catch could be slung over a stick.

I also remember the impersonal attitude towards animal suffering. 'They don't have nerves the same as we do,' was the explanation to my query by which it was all excused. But I was dubious, if still excited, at the way Tom would break a rabbit's leg with me watching – no cries, just overt terror – and then let it go, so that my dog would have the better chance of catching it as it limpingly bounded off across the open field.

My father had even more gruesome tales to tell me about his own indoctrination into sporting ways in the company of Dick Futcher. But I'll drop a curtain over all that.

My dog was Charlotte, a Scottie. Daphne took on many dogs, but she often grew bored with them before they were very old. Her policy then was to give them away, and acquire another. I was the most appropriate recipient for the gift of Charlotte, once her own reign down in the drawing-room was ending. (Nanny acquired a Pekinese called Specks, Cal a Corgi called Honey-bee, and Pip a Pug called Juliana – all in the same fashion.) But I loved Charlotte, in an undemonstrative sort of way. She slept on my bed, and she adored going out rabbiting with me. I took her for granted and she was a much neglected companion, but we appreciated each other's company – for what it was worth.

I was only just beginning to participate in the activities of the local hunts (which consisted of the Wiley Valley and the South and West Wilts) before the outbreak of war disrupted such activities. Cal was thus a far more experienced rider than I ever had the chance to be, but we were both instructed in this art by Charlie Barnes, the head groom at Longleat. I was even blooded at the hunt by John Morrison, who was later to be created Lord Margadale, and his jovial instruction that the blood be left unwashed from my cheeks, no matter how strongly Nanny might protest, was solemnly fulfilled. There are some who wonder if there are still any traces of it there today, since Nanny Marks was always getting accused by my father of under- implementing his instruction that we should all be kept immaculately clean.

I was not particularly sportive in those years – not encouraged to play ball games, or even to feel competitive when running. I suffered from an unnatural fear of heights when out in the woods with Tom Renyard, and I could never climb up to the branches he suggested, to examine a jackdaw's nest or whatever. My biggest achievement over these early years was just in learning how to swim, in the municipal pool at Bath, which I attended quite regularly with Cal.

My first ever sense of sportive achievement did come relatively early, however – when I succeeded in climbing out of my pram, to join Nanny where she was sitting on the lawn. The look of surprise on her face was a delight to behold, so it's a pity that this did not inspire me towards the attainment of more accomplished endeavours. But the truth of the matter is that I was quite a shy and timid child, and quite definitely highly-strung. Not that this featured within my father's own image of what I ought to be, and he did encourage me towards more boyish concerns.

I was only three when Henry decreed that I should be taught how to box – which is curious, perhaps, in that he had never himself indulged in that sport. I was accompanied by Nanny to Macpherson's gym in London, and an instructor showed me how to stand and hold my fists, before advancing step by step towards an opponent, to deliver 'one to the point, and one to the mark'. Having absorbed my lesson, I was matched against another toddler and told to demonstrate what I had learnt. I attempted to do just this. What they had neglected to tell me was that my opponent had been given similar instructions, so that when I moved in close enough to deliver my two punches, I was pre-empted by the receipt of 'one to the point, and one to the mark' – ending up much embarrassed on the floor. And my instructor hastily threw in the towel on my behalf, so as to avoid the additional embarrassment of my bursting into tears.

I was never in fact a cry-baby. Nanny Marks was to tell me (something which I do not remember) that Henry was in the habit of smacking me if I started to cry. So perhaps I became inhibited on that issue. I can remember howling with rage when Nanny refused to give me the toy panda I so desperately desired, or from pain when I fell from a table and bit my tongue. But I certainly wasn't frightened by this boxing defeat, and I remember distinctly that I didn't cry – a fact concerning which the instructor praised me at the time.

There was another aspect to these visits to Macpherson's gym which did trouble me, however. The older boys were always participating in a session of gymnastics when we arrived, right at the end of which came a joy-ride on a merry-go-round – with everyone clinging to rope ladders which revolved. To encourage me in the desire for additional participation, I dare say, the instructor would beckon me down from my seat beside Nanny in the public gallery so that I could join in the fun with them. But I always found that long walk down the aisle from where I'd been enjoying my anonymity to be a cause for excruciating self-consciousness.

I felt myself an intruder into the games of the bigger boys, and that they resented my addition to their throng. But it seemed all too difficult to decline such participation, with Nanny pushing me forward and away from her, urging me not to be shy. All eyes were on me, but I had to start walking. And I developed a dread, in anticipation of that cheery call from the instructor to come down and join them, even though it was impossible to communicate this dread to others.

What I did finally was to summon up my courage, when Henry was driving us all somewhere in his car, to ask if I need go to Macpherson's gym. I am still aware of the deathly silence which greeted this request. Then Nanny hastened to what she imagined was my assistance, by trying to explain to my father how the boys were sometimes a bit rough with me in the boxing. She'd got it all wrong, but I couldn't see how to communicate my true motivation behind the request. I was conscious how there was severe disapproval, and disappointment, in their reaction. But the request was granted, and that put an end to my boxing training – for the time being, in any case.

My father did not always play the role of disciplinarian, although I did suffer from the occasional nightmare on the Big Bad Wolf theme: something to fear, lurking in the shadows, intent on devouring me if it could. His attitude towards me might more accurately be portrayed as one of teasing banter – an idea that I could be chivvied goodhumouredly towards the goals he desired. The bark and the bite were reserved for those occasions when I was failing to respond.

Sometimes there was even a male camaraderie. I was three when he gave me my first sips of port to drink, and my liking for this was to remain with me. It took me long to discern anything wholesome in wine, however, which lacked the former's rich sweetness – and as for beer, I found it insipid and bitter. But I acquired an instant liking for cider when it was first given me by Tom Renyard, and there was a particular occasion not long after that, when I returned home from a night's outing to catch moths by putting treacle on the bark of trees, to receive a severe scolding from Nanny. It couldn't be decided whether I had drunk too much or was suffering from a severe touch of flu.

Returning to the activities that were actually directed by my father, I was just three when I accompanied him to his annual Royal Wiltshire

Yeomanry camp. The colonel had taken his young son to the camp the previous summer, and my father (although only a captain in those days) was damned if he shouldn't follow suit, proud as he was of having a son and heir. I sat beside him in the mess, and was taught by his fellow-officers how to swill my mouth out after a meal – a habit Henry found hard to break once we were back in female society.

What he hadn't bargained on, however, was my delight in sitting on a spectator's chair while the Royal Wiltshire Yeomanry band was rehearsing, and accompanying their music with my own shrill tin whistle. They gave me sixpences to go and buy myself ice creams. But after eating them, I would return to resume my accompaniment, to demonstrate yet once again my appreciation of their band. Daphne was promptly summoned from Sturford Mead to repatriate me within the family fold.

I did display a certain talent for music, nonetheless, being encouraged to join Cal in her piano lessons from Mrs Milner, who arrived by appointment down in the schoolroom. Not that this talent could be described as precocious. And there was no great feeling for music in the family background. Classical records were seldom played, if ever. Daphne's taste was for crooningly fashionable songs like those of Bing Crosby or Fred Astaire, with some jazz and ragtime thrown in for good measure.

Although I was encouraged by Miss Vigers to read such books as the novels of G. A. Henty, I never engrossed myself in such activity. But I was still very young when I appreciated that I ought not to reply 'The Marquess of Bath' in answer to the question of what I intended to become in life. Thenceforward I told people that I would become a writer who illustrated his own books. My talent in drawing had received some praise from Miss Russell, a previous governess. Daphne meanwhile maintained some romantic notions about my emerging as a poet, in the vein of Shelley or Byron, perhaps. So the idea of becoming more or less what I am today was never really that far from my mind.

The first verses that I ever wrote (at the age of seven) were for Daphne, and in the initial two lines of the first one, I stated:

> Oh, the little foal has play,
> while his mother works all day ...

If we accept that I was in some way endeavouring to describe the nature of our own relationship, it stands as admirable evidence for filial devotion, perhaps, but it strikes me today that there may have been a touch of unrealism about my understanding of her activities in life.

Children's parties were very much a part of our lives when we were on the London scene – sometimes at no lesser place than Buckingham Palace. I was instructed by my cousin, Ben Wilson, on how to bow to royalty, and did so with exaggerated grace (not with the head only, as I later learnt to be the more aristocratic way of doing such things). But it was Queen Mary herself who took me by the hand and assisted me to choose my present from the pile of gifts on display. I was ignorant of her special interest in my family at the time, but I certainly regarded her as a dear and dignified old lady.

I was a special favourite, too, of Laura Corrigan, who had been made my godmother. The huge parties she threw were sometimes in my honour, and she was apt to fix the competitions (like the one to see whose gas-filled balloon travelled the furthest) so that I finally heard that I'd won the prize. I remember one little boy complaining that it was unfair because my card was attached to a bunch of four such balloons, whereas his card had merely three. Mrs Corrigan's explanation that I was her godson was ill-received.

I had a special fascination for the conjurors at parties such as these. And my sister (who was a fairy, of course) was on more than one occasion singled out to receive the tame rabbit that got pulled out of a top hat. The day I witnessed a repetition of this trick, but with only a toy rabbit being shaken as it emerged in the conjuror's hand, ranks as the point when I was struck by the idea that the quality of life might be deteriorating.

I was fed with a taste for travel, or at least the expectation of it, while I was still only three. I then accompanied my parents on their trip to Jamaica, on a banana boat called the *Araguaney*. It furnished me with many vivid memories – like the sight of exotic black people, for the first time in my life, along with that of porpoises and flying fish. More important, however, there was a real intimacy with my parents, for both Cal and Pip had been left behind.

I was encouraged to think that, in these travels, I had achieved the real break from infancy. While safely distant from Nanny's arms, Henry had taken me to the barber on board ship and a toddler's curls had been shorn drastically from my head. I can still recollect how Nanny stood there pretending not to recognise me on my return. She was putting her hands over her eyes, exclaiming: 'No, it can't be you! It isn't! Your hair is all in notches.' Perhaps she managed to inspire some inner hankering for a return to long hair, which took some while to find adequate expression.

Activities during the latter part of my childhood were overshadowed by the national preparation for war. After that race back home from Piraillan at the time of the Munich crisis, the momentum towards war became a vivid part of our lives. We had an Austrian cook at Sturford over this period, who had kept a photograph of Hitler ostentatiously on display in the kitchen, and she now went scuttling back home to her native country. Attitudes amongst the rest of the staff were less determinate. Even Nanny had been heard to say that Hitler was probably doing some good things, in bringing the German people back to work. Her comments of ridicule were reserved for Mussolini, and the inflated bullfrog mimicry was one that we all attempted to grasp within our private repertoires. But Munich had made everyone rather more uncertain – a feeling that perhaps we'd been backing the wrong horses, and that it was time to place covering bets elsewhere.

We children were sitting on the paddock gate when Nanny came and told us that war had been declared. I was eating a banana at the time – the last I was to see for quite some number of years. But it didn't feel any too serious at the start. We all knew that we'd never been defeated in a war since the Norman conquest, and even so, I had been led to believe that the Thynne family was descended from those Normans. It wasn't a question of who was going to win, but merely of how long it might last. Surely not as long as the previous one, which had endured for as much as four years?

Henry was now absent from the home scene for lengthy periods, training with the Royal Wiltshire Yeomanry. Sometimes we would go to visit him in camp, even to take up temporary billets with him, in the company of other officers' families. But that was only during the holidays. At other times we had our lessons from Miss Vigers to contend with.

It was only after Daddy had been shipped off to Palestine (to form part of the Eighth Army, which ultimately came into action at El Alemein) that a new sense of urgency took hold. Questions were asked about what we were all doing to assist in the war effort. Mummy was just as enthusiastic as ourselves, drawing up schemes apportioning jobs to each of us. Cal and I were to get up early each morning to feed the chickens, while Daphne was going to do the local milk round, using our pony-cart. But she had second thoughts about the latter chore, and the spare milk from our cows was then diverted towards the manufacture of home-made cheeses, each of which she christened after particular friends or acquaintances. The problem here was that such individuals became emotionally involved with the cheese that bore his or her name, and thus potentially offended at the fate of some of them. They had a knack of getting eaten by the dog, or simply – for whatever reason – being deemed inedible.

Spy stories were rife in the neighbourhood, especially after some garrulous lady accompanied by a meek young man drove up to the front door at Sturford to enquire about the local Home Guard's defence posts. She claimed to have a nervous disposition, and would only consider renting one of our cottages if we could assure her that it was well protected from parachutists. A day or so later, her visit was followed by that of a policeman upon his bicycle. The authorities wanted to question her on the reason for her extensive enquiries, which had yet to result in her renting any place. I retained a vivid memory of what she looked like, but when it was asked if I had taken note of the number-plate on her car, I had to admit that my standard of observation – or of suspiciousness – fell short of what was required in any true patriot. The garrulous lady with her meek young man had either hopped it over the sea to Eire or, more simply, just vanished into the mists of war hysteria.

Bombs far more than parachutists were most to be feared, deep in the heart of the English countryside. And it's a fact that I had long experienced a dread of low-flying aircraft. I have one memory from my days in a pram, waking up to the roar of a biplane as it swooped low over Sturford Mead. Nanny Marks was later to confirm that the occasion which I remembered had in fact occurred. She had always placed the pram under a tree after that, to inspire me with the confidence that they could never swoop that low again. But it may be some residual panic that I still feel when an aeroplane comes too directly towards me.

I was seven at the outbreak of war, and my fear of low-flying aircraft increased for a while, in anticipation of such frequent occurrence. I can remember clinging to the grass on Clay Hill as a bomber made mock strafing runs at a height lower than the point to which I had climbed. It took quite some effort after that for Cal to persuade me to accompany her again on her walks up Clay Hill. She eventually hit upon the solution (suggested to her in an advertisement, which she cut out for my benefit) that those sugar-coated chocolate beans called Smarties are good for a person's nerves. She told me they were bravery pills. So we recommenced our walks up Clay Hill, taking along with us a tube of bravery pills – which were fed to me by the fist-full as soon as the sound of a low-flying aircraft could be heard.

I managed to sleep through the experience of the only high-explosive bomb to be dropped in our immediate vicinity – although Cal heard it all, and was full of exciting detail next morning about how the bomb had whistled while falling, driving her to hide beneath her bedclothes. I didn't even have the daunting recollection of its explosion, despite the fact that it fell just a mile away, slap on top of an isolated garage, opposite the Royal Oak in Corsley, where a man was reputed to have been mending a puncture in his bicycle tyre by the light of an unshielded lamp. He paid for it with his life, and it furnished a cautionary tale for good blackout discipline for many a long night to come.

By 1940 however, we were indeed acquiring some personal experience of the war, in that large hangers for the storage of spare parts for aircraft were being constructed within the Longleat woodlands. And on the suspicion that these might have been ammunition dumps, the area was bombarded with incendiary bombs on two successive nights. Pip and myself acquired one of these toys, on discovering it dangling unexploded from the branches of a tree, to display within our collection of war mementoes – until Mr Gill, the estate agent, persuaded us that it might still be a lethal weapon. It was returned to us, however, after it had been suitably disarmed. I suppose that occasion must rank as the nearest the war ever came to making casualties of us both.

# Chapter 11

## Sex: Unearthing the erotic mould

I felt close to my mother in that somehow, during these early years, I always knew that she loved me the best of all. But it was Nanny whom I declared that I would someday marry – not that she was ever sexy in her behaviour towards me. Quite the contrary, in fact, in that she was quick to rebuke any of us if she thought we might be doing something 'dirty'. She was a tolerant but straight-laced spinster, whom I believe to have been still a virgin to her dying day. She used to tell us that she had once been engaged, but that she discovered he was a bad sort of man. She still wore his gold ring, however, while telling us that she had tried to remove it, but that it was stuck – whereupon Cal produced a hacksaw and severed it from her finger. The very sight of it had provoked feelings of infidelity to ourselves.

In point of fact, there may have been an erotic side to my relationship with Nanny. I shared a bedroom with her – until the arrival of little Baba deprived me of that pleasure. On waking up in the early hours of the morning, I would often transfer myself from my cot to her large bed ... sometimes with wet pyjamas. I have a vivid memory of the delightful warmth of her body when I hitched my leg over her thigh, thus ridding myself of the wet and clammy sensation until it had dried up. She never scolded me for such intimacy, although I'm sure that she was aware what game I was up to. It was something that she permitted me to do because we both liked it.

If it is fair to regard such activity as sexual, then it must be confessed that I was not entirely faithful to her. Nanny had an elder sister called Lizzie, who came on visits and got terribly bossed around. She may have been a trifle on the simple side, and was less outgoing than Nanny – far more the straight-laced spinster. And there were occasions when she stood in for Nanny when the latter was on holiday. But one might have expected that I'd refrain from cocking my leg over Lizzie to dry my pyjamas, even if I did transfer myself to her bed. I can recall how her whole body went stiff, which was in sharp contrast to my previous experience. But she still permitted me to do what I wanted.

With others, however, I was to prove myself quite obstinately faithful to Nanny. I would not permit the nursery-maids to give me a bath, for example. In that respect I regarded my body as being Nanny's alone to touch. The moment the nursery-maid approached me, I would set up a howling cry such as might deter the patron saint of cleanliness – whoever that might be. But my father had decreed that I should submit to his household arrangements, and permit this abuse of my body at the hands of a comparative stranger, also stating the punishment that would be inflicted if I proved disobedient. So when he entered the nursery to discover that I was howling once again, for just that reason, he implemented his threat by banning me from the next family treat – which happened to be my own fourth birthday party.

Nor was I in the least inclined towards infidelity when the usual run of temporary nannies were employed – other than with Lizzie, that is to say. Their behaviour towards me wasn't even remotely sexy, if words of explanation are required, for they were disciplinarians. For example, I disliked baked apple, but there was one of these ladies who would pinch my nose until my mouth fell open (for the purpose of drawing breath) and she would shovel the baked apple into the cavern before I had sufficient opportunity to perceive what she was doing. There was no question of my drying my pyjamas on a lady like that, nor even inviting her to bath me.

There was all the same an additional infidelity when my parents took me on that cruise to Jamaica. I was then given a cabin to share with Evelyne, who was Daphne's lady's maid. My pyjama-drying technique was repeated in her company too, and I recollect that it was an enjoyable experience.

I am not suggesting that I was in some way absorbing any example of infidelity from my mother during this voyage, but I do have a distinct recollection of her flirtatiousness with a stranger (or so I judged him) while we were on board the *Araguaney*. It is, however, a story that's worth telling.

Daphne and I were often seated in the ship's dining-room without Henry yet being present, and I can remember how the man at the table next to ours utilised his games with me to achieve his self-introduction to my mother. It was the game of pretending that his second and third fingers, when extended in my direction, were the twin barrels of an old-fashioned pistol which exploded with a sharp click of his tongue, at the depression of his thumb. We had a lovely pistol battle between the two tables – Daphne distinctly smiling her encouragement – until Henry showed up on the scene.

The point I found personally difficult to comprehend was the way in which Daphne's encouragement for our game was now rapidly withdrawn. I did attempt to continue it, firing several accurate shots in my partner's direction. But Daddy was now looking displeased, and Mummy lent over to whisper that it wasn't a very nice man that I'd been playing with. I was confused as to why attitudes had suddenly changed. The softly coy little expression in her eyes and on her lips had also vanished. Yet somehow Daddy wasn't to be made privy to these changes.

I don't think I associated Daphne's behaviour with sexiness, or even flirtatiousness, and I certainly never thought of her as an appropriate body on which to dry out my wet pyjamas. Indeed, I can only remember one occasion when, during my father's absence, I was actually invited to share her bed, and that was for a single night – even though the original invitation had been for an entire weekend. It didn't work out well for us. She was perpetually waking me up with petulant demands that I cease rolling around in my sleep – to such an extent that I confided to Evelyne next morning that I'd prefer to be put in my father's dressing-room next door. I was concerned not to hurt Daphne's feelings, however, and suggested that the best explanation for the switch of beds was that I didn't like sleeping in pink sheets: a message that was duly delivered – and appreciated.

My relationship with Daphne was an intimate one, notwithstanding. There was no question of my being invited to watch Nanny naked in her bath, but this was quite usual in the case of my mother. She even informed me on how the fountain on a bidet was most properly employed. And when I commented on her breasts, she explained how I had sucked milk from them when I was a small baby – not that this was presented as any privilege special unto myself. Even little Baba was to be permitted that degree of intimacy.

Henry too would invite me to come and chat with him while he was in the bath. So there was never any excessive mystery, or secrecy, about our bodies. I noted how his genitals were that much larger than my own, but this seemed perfectly natural under the circumstances. So were his hands and his feet, for that matter.

I was perhaps more aware how my own sexual characteristics differed from those of Cal – because we had the opportunity to observe each other so frequently in the bath. (Neither 'penis'/'vagina', 'prick'/'pussy' nor 'cock'/'cunt' were yet introduced into our vocabularies.) We required distinctive labels, linguistically, to make it apparent to each other that we had observed such difference. But Cal was never forthcoming as to what she supposed hers might be called. I had my own ideas about mine, however – because Nanny always instructed me to be 'a clean boy' whenever I went to pee. So by association, the thing I did it with became (in my vocabulary) a 'kleenboy'.

Of greater demonstration of the direction in which my sexual orientation was becoming fixed, I should perhaps bring the Zu-Zu twins – more properly known as the Metcalfe twins – into focus. But they were the two little girls, of approximately my own age, who first inspired in me a feeling of possessiveness. They were usually there at the same parties I attended, dressed in long white dresses with scarlet-red sashes. I judged them to be pretty, too. When I was attempting to converse with them, I found myself turning to Nanny to enquire what it was they had said. What it sounded like to me was: 'Zu-zu-zu-zu-zu-zu.' (Hence my private name for them.) Twins have a private language, and this was explained to me – which I found delightfully mysterious, of course. But the idea of other little boys' attempting to interpret what they were saying struck me as an affront to my own identity. So I had a special pained way of watching them when they were doing this to me.

I was still only four when Miss Russell was appointed to be Caroline's governess – several years prior to the advent of Miss Vigers. In sharp contrast to the latter, the former was a youngish, good-looking lady. She may have been even more beautiful than that, for I do seem to remember her as such. I wasn't actually taking lessons from her, but I sometimes sat in with Cal, receiving instruction in drawing and the like. I can remember Miss Russell praising my picture of a blinded Samson pulling down the   pillars of the temple, so perhaps she was reading me stories from the bible as well.

I adored Miss Russell, and she was good with Nanny besides. I can remember us all playing together in the garden at Sturford during the summer of the Abdication crisis, the game being for Mr Baldwin's team to keep King Edward and Mrs Simpson apart. Miss Russell had a good way of combining games with tuition in current affairs. She stimulated me intellectually, quite apart from furnishing me with a visual image for a romantic prototype which was perhaps to recur with some frequency in my life.

She had shoulder-length, blondish hair, and an overt friendliness. (Or was it just that she had a good way with children?) But the relationship was entirely asexual – much as that might be cause for personal regret.

She was only with us for a year. There came a day during the following Christmas visit to Longleat when Nanny informed me sadly that Miss Russell would not be playing with us any more. She had departed, without so much as a hug or a word of adieu. I just rolled on the floor, screaming my head off.

No one explained the situation to me any deeper than that, and it was only years later when I was told, by Aunt Kathleen, how Aunt Emma had reported to my father her seeing the governess accompanying Thomas, my grandfather, on his constitutional walk in the Pleasure Grounds at Longleat – Thomas being a seventy-five year old widower at the time. The idea of Miss Russell's being a suitable governess for us children was no longer a matter to be taken into account ... nor even the idea that the revered head of the family might be entitled to a small romance in the Indian summer of his life. There were now other considerations the clan must have found disturbing – such as the prospect of an additional brood of male-line Thynnes, emerging to grasp some portion of the inheritance from under our very noses.

No, I quite understand that the nubile Miss Russell had to go. I also understand why, in selecting Miss Vigers as her replacement, due notice was doubtless taken of the fact that she was both old and ugly.

My first erotic fantasies were inspired by Charles Kingsley's *The Water-Babies*, which Daphne read to me. I created the fantasy around the visual image of one Susan, whom I met (but hardly ever spoke to) at Captain Olsen's gym in Bath, which we attended for both gymnastic and swimming instruction. All that I can clearly remember is that she had long blond hair and was probably a couple of years older than myself.

What I pictured to myself when I was lying half asleep was that Susan and myself, amongst others, were members of a group of water-babies called 'Livers'. We swam the high seas, naked, while evading the nets of adults, who were fishing for us from above in boats. Their intention was to eat us, yet prior to that they packed us into tins like sardines – where I always found myself packed next to Susan. Escape was invariably devised by my own ingenuity, and we would find ourselves swimming in the depths of the sea once again, naked as ever, and strung out in long chains, the one behind the other, each grasping the one in front. Being the leader of the band, I swam at the head of the chain, of course, and the one immediately behind me was inevitably Susan, grasping me between the legs by the most convenient handle. And thus we swam idyllically, for days and nights on end – until the whole process of capture and escape would get monotonously repeated.

Two points of interest emerge. In that my band of 'Livers' consisted exclusively of little girls, it might be argued that I was already inclined towards polygamy. And in my choice of a name for the band, it derived partly from Cal's expressed opinion that human flesh would probably taste similar to liver, and partly to a predisposition for some existentialist brand of attitude – in the sense of 'living it up', as opposed to waiting to see what might happen to us.

Whether or not I experienced erections during the process of these fantasies is a point I cannot truthfully answer. But there were a whole series of erections, subsequently, which I can accurately date because they occurred while I was in hospital in Bath, suffering from severe mastoid trouble. This came shortly after our return from the holiday in Piraillan, in 1938, when I was six years old.

I had responded to earache by sticking a lead pencil down the offending ear-hole to obtain that deliciously cool scratching sensation upon the inflamed drum – with the result that the infection flared up. Antibiotics had yet to be invented, but the decision to perform a full-scale mastoid operation was delayed for a while, since it was regarded as distinctly dangerous for a young child, and I was, after all, the Thynne family's precious son and heir.

During the period that I was in Bath hospital, I was tended by a nurse to whom I gave the nickname Fuchsia. She wore her hair in two tufts, gathered on each side of her head, which was the fashion in which the Fuchsia fairy was portrayed in a book upon flower fairies that had been read to me by Cal during the period when I believed such creatures to be her kith and kin. I realised how fortunate I was to be cared for so attentively by such a person. I felt close in spirit to her too. Maybe it was the naughty twinkle in her eye, but I have a clear memory of the game that developed during the blanket baths she gave me. While lying there naked, I would provoke her reaction by bringing my penis erect. And she would dab at it with a sponge, exclaiming: 'Oh, you naughty little boy!'

The day came, however, when Fuchsia arrived at my bedside with a solemn face. She told me that although it was quite all right for me to play these games with herself, if some other nurse was to give me a blanket bath, then she might be shocked. I was made to promise that I would reserve this kind of behaviour for herself alone. She had some cause to feel alarmed, for word had come that I was to be transferred to a London hospital for the dreaded mastoid operation. Our secret was safe in my hands, however. The nurse who tended me up in London was a dour Scotswoman, without any manner of naughty twinkle in her eye, and I never felt the remotest urge to erect my penis in her company.

The mastoid operation was successful, incidentally, although there was a period of convalescence during which I was taken by Matron to cheer up the ladies in other private beds. There was one in particular who struck me as beautiful – in her late teens, perhaps, and with long golden hair, reminiscent to me nowadays of the Boticelli *Venus*, whose print did just happen to be framed upon the nursery wall. It was the image of Susan (or even of Miss Russell) reinforced, I dare say. I was taken to sit with her on several occasions, and felt bitterly disappointed when Matron fobbed me off one morning upon a young lady of less angelic appearance. Just one of my stereotypes for attraction had taken root, it might seem, with only limited leeway for divergent types.

It was also during this period of convalescence that I first developed a friendship with my fair cousin, Sally-Anne Vivian (Sal, as she was then called), daughter of Daphne's brother, who was my Uncle Tony. Living in London at that time, she would come and visit me in hospital, and we became particularly friendly. I think we got as far as telling each other that we liked no cousin better. Once again the romantic stereotype was coming together in a fashion to influence my taste in such matters – although there was still plenty of room for additional stereotypes to be implanted over the course of my subsequent history.

I was seven years old when I was first told the facts of life – by Cal, who had just been told them belatedly by her friend Diana Phipps, who had been told them by her brother Nicholas. By the time these facts had been relayed to me, however, they were marginally different from the original instruction. In essence, I was given to believe that I had coagulated from out of my father's urine after he had peed into my mother's womb – which didn't strike me as a particularly nice way for anyone to be conceived. But it was some years before my education in this field was taken any further.

I loved Cal perhaps better than anyone else in the world. She was my most intimate confidante, and our relationship did just occasionally border upon the sexual: watching each other urinate, or the daring examination of each other's genitals perhaps, but nothing more overtly erotic than just that.

With the outbreak of war came my first self-consciously romantic relationship, and this was with Sheila, Lady Milbank, my mother's best friend of that period. Their menfolk had been shipped abroad, to Palestine in my father's case, and our summer holidays were now spent down in Cornwall – initially at a village called Trebetherick, on Hayle Bay.

Sheila was similar to Daphne in many ways: a coyly flirtatious brunette with straight shoulder-length hair and a warmly personal way of chatting and confiding, even with children, so that her subject was made to feel special and uniquely rewarded by her attention. The two of them would play a comic act with me. When I composed a short lyric, in grudging acceptance of the newly imposed war-time diet (of animals trapped by our own gamekeepers), they would perform a little dance around me, singing out the words to me in silly girlish tones.

> Rabbits for lunch, rabbits for tea,
> rabbits are good for you and me!

I decided that I was in love with Sheila, and just before returning home to Sturford, I found a stone which happened to be in the shape of a heart. Daphne was encouraging the liaison, so was happy to buy for me a small tin of glossy red paint, in which colour I immersed my 'heart'. Then I wrapped it in brown paper and left it on her doorstep as a valentine.

On remeeting Sheila some thirty years later, she was to surprise me greatly by taking me upstairs to her bedroom and revealing how she still treasured this heart in a little casket especially dedicated to its preservation. She also disclosed to me at the same time how my grandfather, Thomas, was a little bit romantically inclined towards her over the same period as myself. I certainly wasn't aware of his rivalry at the time; nor do I know if he was aware of mine.

If I was discovering that I exercised a certain charm, and sex-appeal, in some people's eyes, then I was also learning that such an assessment of me was by no means universal. As soon as the bombing of London began, houses in the countryside were invited to volunteer to make room for evacuees. Daphne's generous offer that we should all move into the front of the house, making the nursery and other rooms available for such displaced people, was taken up by a London hospital for crippled children – if only for a short spell. And during those weeks we were indeed deprived of much of our former privacy. Yet by way of compensation, I became slightly enamoured of the young nurse who accompanied these children.

Once again, it was her way with children, I suppose, which was her special attraction. All of those in her care appeared to adore her; and one has to remember that I had been brought up to suppose that I was a superior kind of little boy. So it might have been argued that my chances with her were good, against these – well – invalids. I spent hours with her, for days on end, hoping to obtain her acknowledgement that I had won her admiration, if not her heart.

The young nurse was made of sterner metal than I'd been anticipating, however. None of the remarks I made to her, which were calculated to open her eyes to the fact that I was of superior status to her charges, seemed to be going down very well. 'What a little snob!' was even a comment which I just managed to hear her say. So I eventually tried out the tactic of solidarity, intimating that my mother (not that I really listened to her) had advised me not to play with these children, in case I caught something from them.

Seldom have I found myself so wrong-footed in courtship. The next time I went up to the nursery in search for her, the pretty young nurse was eventually revealed to be hiding behind a door. And it was only shortly afterwards that their hospital decided to transfer them to other premises.

Something that was, just remotely, sinking in upon my consciousness was that other men were more intimate with Mummy than they had been in the past. Daddy's enforced distance from the family scene might have accounted for all that, but there was still a sense of unease in my mind when I went up to her bedroom to kiss her good morning, in the habitual manner, to find one of the men who were staying in the house, standing there beside her bed in a dressing-gown. She also told me, somewhat severely, that I should knock before entering – something she had never required me to do before then. There was a feeling that things were getting out of place within our lives, although it wasn't for myself to analyse what this might be.

The man in the dressing-gown was [X]. He was Daphne's special friend over this period, and I remember how emotional she became when he was wounded in a shooting accident upon Salisbury Plain. Some fighter pilot had mistaken his company on parade as the cardboard targets for his strafing run of machine-gun fire. There were many casualties, and [X] himself was on the danger list for a while. It did enter my mind to wonder if she'd have been equally distressed if we'd been told similar news about Daddy.

Life wasn't quite as it once had been, and we were aware how the war was in some way responsible for all that. But the war was a passing phase, and the family would soon get back into the old rhythm of things. Or that is what I thought at the time.

# Chapter 12

## Identity and Deity:
## The crystallisation of what I am

To examine the beginnings to my life within a more general context: I had indeed been born with a great deal of good fortune heaped there upon my plate – or with the proverbial silver spoon protruding from my mouth. But within the first few weeks of my life I was given some foretaste of things yet to come when some careless visitor managed to drop me on my head. I was taken to hospital for X-ray examination by one Dr H. Graham Hodgson, and his letter, dated 29 August 1932, is still on the family files stating that there was no photographic evidence of fracture or any other injury in the bones of the skull. His certificate makes no mention of the state of the material below the bones of the skull, and there have been some who have wondered about this ever since.

There are some other pictures taken of me at an early age which are indicative of a fierce temper. Or perhaps it just shows how press photographers have always delighted in snapping me at my worst. But Nanny Marks in any case did carry that impression of me as a fierce-tempered baby, setting it in contrast to the milder temperaments of the other children.

I don't think I was a spoilt child in the sense of having everything my own way. The very fact of having a sister nearly four years older than myself would have been sufficient to kill that prospect, even if it had been there. From the time when I had a specific memory of myself (which dates from before my third birthday) it was developing on the lines that I was someone both loved, and loving, but more essentially as someone who was important in life.

I still maintain an image of me as a lovable child – for all the reasons which seemed to appeal so much to my mother at the time. But I might choose to single out what I now regard as the quality of candour, or direct openness, in all my relationships. It was to be gradually debased, of course. I was no longer being quite so straightforward in my relationship with Miss Vigers, for example. In that case, my behaviour might even have been described as hypocritically affectionate, to suit my more devious ends. And to some extent, it may be that all qualities turn out to be corruptible, although I like to think that there is still something of that original Me that remains intact.

Another essential aspect of me is that I was highly-strung. The way in which this first came vividly to my own attention (if only retrospectively) was on our way to Jamaica, on board the Araguaney. When it came to the practice boat drill, we had all been lined up on deck, waiting for the ship's hooter to blow. But when it did, I jumped out of my skin, with my leg shooting up uncontrollably as if in some manner of weird salute. The idea of the next boat drill was something which thereafter I dreaded – and there have been similar experiences throughout my life.

There is also the concept of humour to consider. The urge to laugh (if indeed it was initially present) was never cultivated during my early child-hood. I was a solemn little boy, always endeavouring to interpret what hap-pened to me, or whatever might be said to me, quite literally. That 'imp's trick', when I was invited to watch smoke appearing from my father's ears, may have been an example of Henry's humour, but it never became an example of mine. There was always something not quite in tune between the two of us as to what humour should really entail. And if Daphne was good at exploding into sympathetic mirth when others were displaying their humour for her appreciation, she was not tuitional concerning what it was in life that had the merit to be regarded as funny.

I don't think Cal had a particularly well-developed sense of humour either, but she was in a far better position to pontificate upon the subject of what it was all about. She would explain to me with dead-pan serious-ness of expression why the cartoons in the *Daily Mirror* were funny. (That and the *Daily Express* were the family's daily reading.) I remember a series of cartoons which went under the heading of 'Sillystrations': one in partic-ular depicted a man whose fingers were removed from his hand and plant-ed in his hair – to illustrate the absurdity in the English language of saying 'He ran his fingers through his hair.' Cal laboured long in trying to make me understand why this should make me laugh. But she finally endorsed the parental verdict that I must have no sense of humour. It was a label which stuck with me in the family for many a long year to come.

Alongside the concept of identity which was forming, we should also consider how I was beginning to relate myself to the universe as a whole – or, as some might prefer to phrase it, beginning to conceive God. Religion wasn't regarded as an important subject by either of my parents. But they had conformed with tradition by having me christened and furnishing me with godparents, most of whom died during my infancy. The one stalwartly remaining, however, was Laura Corrigan, who delighted in the social elitism of being so openly related to a future marquess.

She took her duties seriously too, in that she persuaded Daphne that I ought to be read stories from the Bible. Obedient to the godmother's bidding, she did so – from a beautifully illustrated book donated by Laura for that purpose. I grew up quite well versed in these matters, although it wasn't until she started giving children's parties for my benefit that my appreciation for Mrs Corrigan took firm root. Indeed, there is one terrible story of how, as an infant after she had taken me up in her arms, I gave way to a temper tantrum and seized her by the hair – which happened to be a wig. But I could hardly have been expected to comprehend such matters at the time.

Religion gets muddled up with superstition, of course, and I was fed an abundance of that within all the legendary concerning Longleat – quite apart from the fact that my sister happened to be a fairy. I believed in ghosts, and I believed in Father Christmas – until Ben Wilson informed me that it was just a question of grown-ups making fools of us. I was five at the time, and felt grossly deceived, insisting that he wasn't telling me the truth. Ben was hastily banished from our Longleat nursery to his own, but Cal did gently open my eyes to the fact that the real world was as he had stated.

There was no way that I was going to remain a gullible ninny, now that my eyes had been opened. We were friendly (up until then) with the Wills family, of fame for their manufacture of cigarettes, and they were taking us all in a convoy of cars to the local pantomime in Bath. Their daughter Caroline was just a few months older than me, and we had been seated next to one another in their own car – perhaps even with marital prospects in mind. But I blotted my copybook by passing on to her this recent information I had received, which went down far worse in her case than in my own. She was screaming so loudly, in fact, that the convoy had to be halted so that I could be removed from my seat of honour and deposited in a vehicle for remainders which travelled at the back of the procession.

My sense of disillusionment didn't cease there, however. When Nanny took us out shopping in Harrods, to assist in the task of choosing our Christmas presents, she attempted to revive my faith in the existence of Father Christmas by pointing him out to me and urging me to queue up with the other little children to tell him what I wanted. I was reluctant to do as she urged, because I now knew that they were all making a fool of me. But I was nudged up on to his dais, and whispered in his ear that I knew, really, that he didn't exist. I can remember a pained expression upon his face, but my memory doesn't serve me with his verbal retort.

It was Cal more than anyone else who kept my sense of religion alive. She was a convinced believer at that time, exemplifying an eldest child's natural inclination to promote such attitudes – because the recognised existence of God might endorse the logic within other aspects of a hierarchy which suited her, in some respects, very well. But there is no way in which our upbringing could, in reality, have been labelled as religious.

Even so, I said my prayers regularly, although I worried about the way in which they should cover everything. There was some philosophical thinking which emerged behind all this – which boiled down to an intellectual search for identifying the very hub of life. And I do remember asking God to give me a happy life, which I considered might cover just about everything.

But I also asked for fame. And when I discussed with Cal the subject of what our prayers rightly should cover, she pointed out that most people who are famous after their death weren't at all famous during their lifetime. So which kind did I want? And having given the matter due consideration, I settled for the posthumous version – which has irked me ever since, in that I was subsequently to become far more hungry for instant renown.

That wasn't quite all, however, for there was still the question to be determined of the age at which I should finally decease. This too was something to be debated with Cal quite openly before I put it into my prayers. We didn't much like the idea of a doddery senility, but we certainly didn't want to die young. I think that we set the desirable age limits between sixty and ninety, although I now find myself wishing that we'd set the upper limit far higher.

I was also much intrigued by the notion of causation. It struck me that my whole future life's history would diverge, irretrievably, from one course to another if, for example, I picked up a particular stone from the ground in front of me instead of walking past it and then turning ... left? ... Or perhaps even right? The trivia within such detail became obsessive at times.

Miss Vigers should be praised for introducing me to an interest in astronomy. But I think it originated in my sincere marvelling at the sight of the star-studded sky, which Cal and I used to creep outside to watch, combined with the secrecy of stealing food at night from the refrigerator. My interest in the stars was noted (from my questions) by Miss Vigers, who then read us a boring book on the subject. The interest survived.

Miss Vigers also took us regularly to church on a Sunday morning – the one in Corsley, next to the house where Sir John Thynne had once lived. It was a social exercise as far as she was concerned, all part of the correct upbringing for members of the county establishment, on the fringes of which she herself played her role. But I don't suppose that our presence in the congregation was greatly appreciated, for Cal and I spent much of our time working up fits of church giggles. Our parents, I noted, only saw fit to include themselves in such religious devotion at Christmas and at Easter.

Henry had been made to swallow a surfeit of religion in his youth by his mother, Violet, the Christian Scientist, but it was all part of the general release after the First World War that he felt a sense of mockery for much that he had previously regarded as holy. I can remember him telling me when I was seven that he didn't believe in God, and nor would I once I had grown to be a man. 'It's women who believe in God.' An association was thus suggested to my mind that atheism was linked to my required development as a macho male. Caroline, who overheard the conversation, insisted to me later that I should not heed his words. But then she was a woman, wasn't she?

So what had happened to me over these past first nine years of my life? Let me now review the situation, placing my full personal identity within the situation that I have described.

I had been born within the last decade of peace within Europe, but I had also experienced the outbreak of war. I had been given acquaintance of both environments, and they were starkly in contrast to each other. The spell of peacetime had furnished me with a personal taste of what life had been like, at Longleat, during the last declining years of what others seemed to regard as its golden age. I held Longleat and all that it stood for in awe, and I had witnessed the clan gatherings at Christmas time, with a relatively large domestic staff to take care of their welfare. I knew of the expectations, even the optimism, that it was all going to continue just like that *ad infinitum*. Even so, this was an epoch to which I was never subsequently able to feel that I belonged. The real Me was to start, I think, with the impact of the war and its aftermath.

# PART THREE

# LUDGROVE (1)

# Chapter 13

## Career:
## Adjusting to a school environment

The idea of being packed off to a boarding school when I was just nine years old was never a prospect that I regarded with too much apprehension. There was always the new status of becoming a schoolboy to consider, which was definitely one up on being taught privately at home.

Miss Vigers herself was the first to encourage me to think of things that way, and she was partly responsible for the choice of Ludgrove as the preparatory school to which I should be sent, for she was well versed in such matters. One of her previous charges was already at Ludgrove, which had recently emerged as the most fashionable place for the sons of the aristocracy and their entourage to be educated. It specialised in the idea of preparing boys for getting into Eton. Run by Mr Barber, who had captained the Yorkshire cricket team prior to becoming a headmaster, the emphasis was upon leadership qualities and sporting excellence rather than upon anything quite so mundane as scholastic ability.

I had the misfortune of being in quarantine for mumps at the beginning of May 1941, when all the other new boys were settling in. So I was very much the newest boy when Daphne finally drove over to Ludgrove (using up some portion of her precious petrol ration) to deliver me safely into Mr Alan Barber's hands. Mr Barber was known as Ali by nickname, of course.

I remember the moment of separation, both of them expecting that I was going to burst imminently into tears. I think that Daphne would have felt flattered if I had, but then the essential conditioning from Henry had

always been much against such behaviour. That first instance of total isolation from the rest of the family is indeed quite a psychological trauma for
any little boy, and I certainly felt a lump in my throat. But I didn't let go
of my emotions, and as soon as Mummy and the car were out of sight, Mr
Barber led me gently indoors to come and meet some of the other new boys
– of whom there were eight.

It wasn't until about a year later that Mr Barber made any comment
upon this moment of separation, and then it was only indirectly. He was
talking to a whole group of us, although I knew he wanted me to appreciate that he was referring to myself. He told us that he always knew if a boy
was going to settle in well at Ludgrove, from the moment of watching him
say goodbye to his mother. If he didn't burst into tears, he knew that everything would be fine.

I think it's true to say that Mr Barber and I attained a good working
relationship from that very instant.

Ludgrove was a large Victorian building with long corridors and spacious classrooms, and among other delights the extensive grounds contained playing fields and avenues of rhododendrons. There was both farmland and woods in the vicinity, fairly reminiscent of the countryside at
home, although it all seemed flatter in this Berkshire landscape near
Wokingham. The town itself was a good mile away, and there were few
other houses before one reached it. It all furnished a sense of peace and
seclusion, in considerable contrast to the fact that we were all at war.

There were others at Ludgrove whom I had met previously – like the
Morrison brothers, James and Charlie, with whom we had shared a house
in Norwich for a while during the weeks of final training for the Royal
Wiltshire Yeomanry, just prior to their embarkation for Palestine.

Morrison Minor was almost exactly the same age, and I had developed
an unhealthy respect for him in that he had floored me in a friendly
wrestling contest while we were still at Norwich.

Then there was Peter Munster, some two years older than me, who was
the son of Peggy, who had been Daphne's best friend at one of those
schools from which she had been expelled. Munster had obviously been
instructed to keep a watch over my interests, to see that I found my feet all
right. So I regarded him in some manner as an elder brother.

But the crucial task at the outset of my school career was to find out
how well I got on with my peer group of contemporaries, and I experienced my due share of problems. Most of the 'new kids' were housed by
tradition in Dormitory 27, whereas the eldest of the 'early-bedders' were in

Dorm 8. There was an atmosphere of mild bullying in their way of asserting their dominance over our group, hitting us with bath towels, or flicking us with their neck ties whenever we passed the open door of their dormitory in our pyjamas after taking the compulsory evening bath – making us run for it or take the treatment they handed out to us.

We were quite scared of them in that they were both senior to, and slightly bigger than, ourselves. But we wanted to get even with the whole bunch of them. Getting even was a matter of reflating our own egos after such continual deflation at the hands of these louts. So I came up with an idea (which I thought bright at the time) of drawing ugly faces on separate pieces of paper, labelling each with the name of one member from their gang – printed in capital letters to retain anonymity – and then posting them individually beneath the lid of their particular classroom desks.

So far so good – but I hadn't been counting on their organising a systematic testing of our handwriting in capital letters, with the requirement to make a copy of one of the ugly faces I had drawn, plus an oath on the holy Bible that we were not ourselves responsible for the outrage.

Exposure seemed imminent when someone who wasn't even in our dormitory declined to take his oath on the holy Bible on the grounds that it would be against his religious scruples. So their suspicion was pointed in his direction, he fiercely protesting his innocence all the while. Doubts set in, and the gang finally lost interest in their investigation. My sense of relief was enormous, since I realised how close I had been to exposure and the punishment that might have been inflicted by the thugs of Dorm 8.

Images are fluid at the outset of school life. Everyone waits for you to do something that they begin to regard as 'in character', so that expectations may thus be formed that you will continue to act in the same way. My own such achievement was on the cricket field, towards the end of this, my first summer term.

This is not a tale of sporting prowess, for it took me several more years before I reached double figures as a batsman, or even managed to bowl with any artifice. Because I was slow to react, however, to the approach of cricket balls struck with velocity in my direction, there were quite a number of occasions on which I held my ground, permitting the missile to strike me on the body rather than endeavouring to take effective evasive action.

The climax of the cricket season arrived when the school was divided up into teams which played one another. Points were obtained for a win, and prizes for the ultimate victors. 'Cabbage' Reed (so named because of his flat, as opposed to cauliflower, ears) was one of the masters who regularly umpired these games, and he was evidently much impressed by my 'guts' as a fielder. He drew the team captain's attention to this quality which he thought he perceived in me, and in spite of the fact that I was only a mere new kid, I found thereafter to my intense discomfort that I was regularly placed at mid-on, where the school's hardest sloggers slammed the cricket ball through the vain defences of my outstretched arms, to strike whatever portion of my body might happen to be in the line of fire.

I didn't enjoy this introduction to the game of cricket, but I did manage to acquire a reputation for guts within the school that was spread around by the comments of Cabbage Reed.

As far as scholastic work was concerned, I didn't do as well at the start as Miss Vigers had been predicting for me. Or let us call it an average performance. Although there were few mistakes in what I did, I was excruciatingly slow, so lost marks on the quantity of unfinished work. Too much attention had gone previously into the neat presentation of all that I did, which was performed in a spirit of methodical thoroughness rather than in any competitive race against the clock – a skill essential to acquire for those who succeed in our contemporary world.

It is also true to say that I didn't take kindly to the personality of the teacher in whose hands we had been placed. He delighted in taking an offending pupil by the ear and twisting it sadistically while he delivered his corrective comments. I have always been sensitive to the attainment of personal sympathy with the person who had been appointed to instruct me, and this kind of treatment didn't encourage such a thing to happen.

Over subsequent terms I got the hang of working faster – at the expense of tidiness – and my competitive edge improved. But the tenor of the praise which I thus merited was directed more towards my enthusiasm than towards any special scholastic ability. And it always depended upon who was teaching me for me to obtain the best results. I felt an undoubted rapport with Cabbage Reed, and always did well under his tuition. But Ludgrove was undergoing the traumatic experience of losing most of its best (younger) teachers over this period, as they were called up for war service – to be replaced on some occasions, and for the very first time in the school's history, by women. None of us were quite sure what to think about that.

One of the new arrivals was Mr Durnford, who was enthusiastic about introducing new ideas into the school. (He survived for less than a year within this highly conventional environment.) I was somewhere near the bottom of his French class, and felt no great urge to do much better. But one day he walked in and started firing IQ tests at us, verbally, although it was only afterwards that he explained what he had been up to. He would ask the question, and then pause to see how many hands were raised before singling out one of us to reveal the answer we had in mind. Because my hand was frequently raised, I was pleased to have the question tossed in my direction many times. And his verdict to the class, on reaching the end of his experiment, was that a teacher invariably discovers that there is someone sitting near the bottom of the class who does far better than those sitting near the top.

In my school report of that term, he was the first teacher to suggest that I was considerably more intelligent than my performance at school revealed.

Mr Barber, who was himself pedantically slow and painstaking in his methods of tuition, never agreed with this verdict, and delivered his own less flattering assessment next term – informing my parents that hard as I tried, I wasn't the brightest of pupils. Nonetheless, I was always one of his favourites, for it must be admitted that he displayed an unwavering admiration for the British aristocracy. We somehow exemplified the qualities that he wanted to instil into others, and wherever we might fall short of those standards, he was inclined to accept our personal excuses.

When Mr Barber spoke to the assembled school on the subject of the character development he regarded as important for all to acquire at Ludgrove, the emphasis was upon gentlemanly conduct, plus a warning that we must learn to pull our own weight. The days when the fruits of life were all handed to us on a silver platter were now past. We had the privilege to come from well-to-do families, and to be receiving our education 'in the best school in England'. Elitism was definitely preached to us, even if that word was never used.

Although I displayed little genuine talent at either cricket or football – sporting activities in which Ludgrove's reputation ranked supreme among the local preparatory schools – I did make my mark in various other similar fields. Small triumphs in swimming and gymnastics, in which I displayed an ability to compete on better than level terms, and, a more significant one, in boxing, where that early training in Macpherson's gym on how to deliver 'one to the point, and one to the mark' finally gave me an edge over those who were matched against me. I developed a neat little left jab, and my reputation for guts served me well in deterring any of the school thugs from premeditated aggression.

Tuition in both music and art at Ludgrove was uninspired, and my ability in each of those fields stagnated over the next few years. But I was discovered to have a beautiful treble voice when singing, and solo parts were thrust upon me at the school concerts – performances that gave me many butterflies in the stomach before I had to go on stage.

I was, however, making a small reputation for myself as a storyteller. Although it was forbidden to talk after the lights had been switched out, depending upon whom the dormitory monitor might be, there was quite a lot of whispered conversation during the early hours of the night. It was often the case that a dormitory would produce its 'professional' storyteller, so designated by popular acclaim. And the ghost stories about Longleat opened up into other fanciful sagas with a savour of Edgar Allan Poe. I displayed some talent in this field, and I benefited from the popularity which derived therefrom.

Indeed, I was not an unpopular young schoolboy. During my very first term I had heard myself being described by those just a little older than myself as 'the most decent of the new kids'. Decency at Ludgrove was a much-esteemed quality. I lacked the sporting prowess to emerge instantly at the forefront of school attention, but my school reports all indicated that I had settled in well, which could be regarded as an encouraging start to my career.

# Chapter 14

## Siblings: The difference in being a schoolboy

Now that I was at Ludgrove, the question arose as to whether Caroline should continue her education with Miss Vigers or be sent off to boarding-school like myself. Nobody liked Miss Vigers, so a decision was taken to send her to 'Mrs Ffyfe's' at Longstowe Hall, which was in vogue at that time as the girls' school with the most fashionable snob-appeal, and once again with an emphasis upon social airs and graces rather than upon scholastic eminence. She was becoming a schoolgirl, in fact, a couple of terms later than I had become a schoolboy. But the age-grouping at her place set it as the equivalent of Eton, as opposed to a mere preparatory school.

The fate of Miss Vigers was now sealed.

Nanny made heavy use of the argument that Chris (who was now in the process of shedding the name Pip) was terrified of the old dragon and would never manage to learn anything at all under her tuition. Far better that he should go to school locally, in Warminster, returning home to Nanny's loving arms each evening, than to suffer so much in the school-room at Sturford. Daphne too was sympathetic to the idea of such an outcome, and it was she who had to make the decisions now that Henry was in the Middle East.

In point of fact Miss Vigers finally cooked her own goose. The situation unfolded thus.

During my second term at Ludgrove I had written a letter to Daphne enquiring if Nanny and Miss Vigers were still fighting as bitterly as ever – ending with a hideous caricature of what I suggested the latter looked like. (I was drawing a whole lot of ugly faces at this time – like the ones I had inserted into the desks of those sleeping in Dorm 8.) Daphne unfortunately left my letter lying on her desk in the drawing-room where Miss Vigers spotted it, and read it. If she had been wise, she would have kept the fruit of her nosiness to herself – but she was unable to resist the satisfaction of complaining to her employer about the attitudes she (Daphne) encouraged in her children. I had always been the great favourite of Miss Vigers, so she now made it clear just how wounded she felt by the caricature I had drawn.

I heard nothing of the business directly from Miss Vigers. It was Daphne who warned me about what had happened, when she came down to Ludgrove to take me out for the day. (That happened regularly once a term, and those boys who received more attention from their mothers than this were regarded by Ludgrovians as distinctly cosseted.) She advised me that I had best try to placate Miss Vigers by writing her (Miss Vigers) a letter ending up with an ugly caricature of herself (Daphne). In this manner the old harridan might conclude that my artistry was really quite harmless, and that it was directed even against those whom I loved the most.

So I did as Mummy suggested.

Poor Daphne then had to undergo the unpleasant experience of having Miss Vigers bring my letter for her to read, crowing viciously over what she supposed must rank as my mother's humiliation. It was an instance of course of winning a battle while losing the war, in that my mother was now that much more eager to side with Nanny once the redundancy issue had been suggested.

Although I had already been fully informed of all that had occurred, Miss Vigers requested that I should not be told about her imminent departure until after the event, so that we could spend a last few idyllic days together on my return from Ludgrove for the Christmas holidays, before she packed her bags and left. The fact that I went along with this hypocritical charade is not much to my credit.

Chris was now signed up locally with the Lord Weymouth School in Warminster – the one that had been founded by the 1st Viscount at the instigation of Bishop Ken. But he still failed to make adequate progress, perhaps because his attitude had already been soured in that direction. I was finding, however, that he furnished a companion in boyishness such as Cal could never provide. And despite my love for her, it did strike me that she was becoming more and more girlish with every additional term that she spent at Mrs Ffyfe's.

Cal was different because she was a girl, and I never really felt myself to be in direct competition with her. Moreover, there were whole areas in the relationship which were still beneficial to both of us. It was the elder-sister-cum-mother game that she played. I would confide in her in a way I would never confide in anyone else. And she would read to me from books that she herself had enjoyed. She was far more into literature, as a subject, than I was.

Cal was apart, and I didn't feel myself to be in rivalry with her. But when it came to Chris, I always felt confident that he was no real match for me when it came to an assessment of our mother's proportionate affection. I can remember an episode which stands as evidence to that effect.

Daphne was up in the nursery at tea time, chatting with Nanny at the table, while Chris and I were playing with tin soldiers near by. Although engrossed in our game, I still had half an ear cocked upon their conversation, and I heard Daphne enquire softly which of the two of us Nan preferred. Nan began to explain earnestly that she always felt that Chris was the more in need of protection than Alexander – whereupon they must have observed that I was listening. Daphne caught my eye, and I distinctly heard her softly say: 'Well you can have him!'

This told me nothing I didn't already know, with regard to Daphne's regard for me, but I did feel offended in that I had now learnt where Nanny's preference lay, and I remember tackling her on the subject later – receiving much the same explanation that she had already given. When badgered on the subject, she was apt to say that her preference amongst us was for Caroline, 'because she's the only little girl that we have'. But it was obvious to us really that her protective instincts were invariably attached to whomever was the youngest of the brood.

Valentine, who was finally obliged to shed the name Baba to become Val (somewhat under protest, however, since he appreciated the advantages of being the youngest in the family), was now beginning to emerge as a personality in his own right. What we didn't greatly appreciate in him was an element of smugness. He was Nanny's favourite, and revelled in that status. Sitting beside her for meals at the nursery table, he waited with a confident little grin on his face until she sliced some extra piece of bacon (or whatever) from her own plate to place it upon his – theoretically without the rest of us noticing what she had done. But there was strict food rationing for things like bacon, so we invariably did notice, and were fierce in our protests about such favouritism. And Val would irritate us greatly with his constantly repeated catch-phrase: 'Let Nanny do as she likes!'

There was something in our hearts that represented a criticism of Val that he had everything up in the nursery too easy for him, and that the nursery was the only environment that he knew. It seemed as if he was developing an attitude that he only had to smile sweetly, and Nanny would come rushing to his assistance. We had the feeling that he ought to learn rapidly that life at school, if not subsequently, would never turn out to be quite so simple as that.

Then came an atrocious example (as we saw it) of how life seemed to be dishing out undeserved rewards to Val. He had just mastered the art of rowing the dinghy on Sturford pond, although he was not permitted to do so unless he had an adult with him. So he persuaded Mrs Sims, the house-keeper, to let him take her for a spin in the boat. He was the first to climb into his seat, and sat there while she attempted to transfer her weight from the foot on the bank, to the foot in the boat. Unfortunately he didn't wait long enough, and on heaving away from the shore, he caused Mrs Sims to perform the splits so that she ended up in the freezing water – and neither of them could swim. Val did attempt to haul her from the water, but she was a solid little lady and his strength proved insufficient. All that he could do was to twine the mooring chain around her neck, and then run off to fetch adult assistance.

He was convinced at the time that we should all be furious with him for what he had done. Having reported where Mrs Sims was to be found (although he did not specify whether above or below the surface of the water), he made himself very scarce. It took Nanny a good hour to find his hiding-place. He had managed to squeeze himself under Daphne's bed, and was discovered only because his feet could be seen protruding on the far side.

What none of us had anticipated was the way everyone who heard about Val's exploits sang his praises. It seemed to be forgotten that he should never have dumped Mrs Sims in the pond in the first place. Instead, he received commendations on rescuing her. I know not how, but it even got into the press, who billed him as a little hero who had saved an elder-ly lady who couldn't swim from drowning. And then he had fan mail from other elderly ladies who couldn't swim – some even enclosing money with their letters. There was no justice in the world.

After that came another episode which enhanced the notion that Val had a personality of his own. Once the worst of the blitz had come to an end, the Battle of Britain having been won, we were on rare occasions allowed to stay the night up in London. One such occasion was for the marriage of my Uncle Douglas, Daphne's half-brother. Our family went up to stay overnight at the Savoy Hotel. I cannot remember the circumstances, but Val was refusing to do what he had been told to do, and had locked himself in the bathroom so that nobody (not even Nanny) could discuss the matter more forcefully with him. And this situation was prolonged to the point when it became necessary to telephone for the assistance of the house carpenter, to remove the hinges from the door so that Valentine could be extracted from his sanctuary. But when the realisation of such humiliating public exposure had sunk in, and while the carpenter was already preparing to perform his task, Val simply unlocked the door and rejoined the assembled company – causing us all to feel far more foolish than little Val.

Then came the term that Chris was to accompany me back to Ludgrove, and of course I was greatly excited about that. I would be known as Thynne Major, for one thing. Having a Minor was always regarded as an asset when it came to status, and I played out my new role with some zest – by which I probably mean that I became bossy to an extreme.

I was genuinely concerned, however, that my Minor should make a good start to his school career. And around this time I was endeavouring to enhance my own image amongst my peer group at Ludgrove by indulging in those activities that were expressly forbidden – night-prowling in particular.

This was a matter of getting up in the middle of the night and creeping down to the kitchens to steal food.

There was one individual called Stevenson, who was currently riding on the crest of a wave in popularity because he had scooped out the middle of a blancmange, due to be served up next day at the headmaster's table, from underneath, so that his enterprise would go undetected until someone put a spoon into it. But the severe 'swishing' that Steve had ultimately received – on being caught in the act of making hideous noises upon the chapel organ (supposing that such music would be attributed to the school ghost) – did not seem to act as the deterrent to others which had been intended.

There was still a whole group of us who aspired to emulate such daring, and I felt that I was only furnishing the most desirable fraternal influence when introducing Chris, at the outset of his school career, to such activities. So we set out one midnight, (just four of us) to raid the kitchens.

The main danger to be overcome was that Spook – who was Mr Barber's elderly cocker spaniel – was apt to wake up and start barking. And that is precisely what happened on this occasion. We hid ourselves in the music room, trembling at the prospect of instant retribution, and we did hear Mr Barber's slippered feet go padding past the door of the music room to catch red-handed whoever might be discovered in the act of raiding the kitchen.

It was a long wait, with hearts pounding, until the slippered feet came back past us once again, on their way up to Mr Barber's own bedroom. Then we slunk back by another staircase each to his own dormitory, all of us much relieved to have escaped detection. It was only next morning that one of our group confided to me that my Minor had displayed the most intelligent of reactions.

'There was a big puddle where he was hiding. He peed on the carpet.'

And that way I've no doubt that Spook received the punishment that he deserved.

I was certainly proud of having a Minor, and I dare say that my disposition of authority over him might well have been evident, at the time, for all to see. I know that Daphne was irritated by it on an occasion when she came down to visit us. As I see it, I was just being schoolboyish – walking a few yards ahead of her with Chris, and displaying (I suppose) just how concerned I was to reveal my independence of spirit, and the new *entente* between my younger brother and myself.

For whatever reason, Mummy was offended and gave me a petulant lecture about my not seeming to appreciate how she'd come all this way to see me, and I wasn't giving her my full attention. But it was worse than that. She told me that there were men who regarded her as being one of the most beautiful women of her generation. I didn't seem to realise how lucky I was to have her as my mother. I did owe a lot to Daphne, and I was fully aware of this.

But there was an unease now developing within me that things weren't quite right within our relationship.

# 15

## Parents: The marriage quakes

Both of my parents were to assure me, in later years, that there had been nothing wrong with their marriage prior to the war. Daphne has admitted to me that there was one short affair (with a famous film actor), but she was leaving me to suppose, on that occasion, that the rest had been just flirtation. She was to qualify this line in a subsequent conversation by telling me how she had been seduced (somewhat against her inclination) by the father of a schoolfriend of mine. But she added that she went home and told Henry all about it, and that the incident was promptly put behind them. 'That was the way we settled such matters,' she confided.

When I was having a similar conversation with Henry, he displayed some doubts about the degree of Daphne's fidelity, but was still adamant that the marriage had been all the success it was proclaimed to be in the eyes of society at large. Yet he also stated that he used to feel uncomfortable on their social outings together, in that Daphne (by way of contrast) appeared so much at home within such large gatherings, with an effervescent ease in conversation, whereas he regarded himself as being excruciatingly shy in those circumstances – essentially tongue-tied unless people came up to talk to him about himself. The modest side of him could never permit him to believe that people might be interested in his personality as such rather than in the aura of Longleat which, if they knew about it, surrounded him.

Stuck out there in the Middle East, and without any special admiration for ladies other than the type he met on the London social scene,

Henry's sex-life was non-existent. Or in point of fact he told me once that he reverted to masturbation.

But the situation in Daphne's case was of course very different. There was a different attitude prevailing now from what there had been in peace-time. The men you escorted might well be on the casualty list tomorrow, so every occasion was regarded potentially as (for them) the last chance. They had best enjoy life while still they might. And it was all part of the war effort, so to speak, for British women to ensure that their menfolk went to war in a satisfied frame of mind. They would fight better that way, potentially to protect those they left behind from the barbaric ravages of invading Huns.

Daphne had always been renowned as a vivacious party hostess, and this reputation did not fail her in time of war. Sturford Mead became a haven for officers training in the vicinity (at Warminster, Tilshead, Lulsgate and such places) to receive relaxing entertainment over a weekend's leave. A small succession of infidelities may have occurred during this period. But Daphne herself was to tell me later that these situations were more likely to occur up in London. It was a question of getting caught by an air raid when you were in someone else's house. It then became desirable to find some pleasant way of passing the enforced period of house detention.

Sometimes it was just a matter of playing little games, devised by those who had been entrapped in such a lair. Daphne had much praise for Prince Dimitri Romanov (who was to marry Lady Millbank after her own husband had been killed) in the games that he organised. For example, there was a game called 'Sweeties'. He required everyone to pour the pills from any bottle that they carried into a hat. The contents were then redistributed at random, and swallowed immediately. Subsequent behaviour, if any different from that usually displayed, could then be attributed to the mixture of unknown drugs – without fault attributable to themselves.

I knew nothing at all about Daphne's London scene. The blitz of night-bombing was in progress, so we were never permitted to remain up there overnight. But I did see something of the weekend parties at Sturford, which never really struck me at the time as posing any threat to the stability of our family unit. And in all probability the highest jinks were reserved for those periods when her eldest children were away at school. But we knew there had been rowdy parties during our absence, and on one occasion we learnt how the drawing-room had caught fire during the night, undergoing considerable damage. At the height of the blaze an air-raid warden had phoned to complain that the house was showing its lights.

Some of those at Sturford thrived upon the new libertine atmosphere, and none more than Mrs Sims – or 'Simbags', as Daphne had now affectionately dubbed her. The dinnertime guests were no doubt generous to her, and she knew how to solicit their tips with impromptu cabaret performances. It was a matter (as I've since been told) of her rushing in when the port was on the table, wearing any item of military uniform that might have been left upon the hall table, to give her own genuinely Cockney if not strictly authentic version of *Knees up, Mother Brown* – or whatever. It all added to the desired atmosphere in which everyone let their hair down, so her acts were invariably well appreciated.

Details were sparse as to what might be happening to Henry, out there in the Middle East. We gathered that he was not yet in action, so it came as a bit of a surprise to me when someone at Ludgrove (who was reading all that was available in the papers about the current battle of El Alamein) enquired if my father was called Viscount Weymouth and, on my confirmation, showed me a piece of a few lines which stated that he had been wounded. A wound can be anything, even as light as a scratch, so I did not feel unduly perturbed. I had the feeling that if it had been serious, Mummy would have seen fit to tell me about it before it had appeared in the papers.

When Mr Barber did in fact call me aside after school lunch, as he imagined, to break the news to me in the gentlest possible manner, I was smiling throughout – as befits an occasion when a pupil discovers that he already knows something his teacher assumes he does not. The poor man was quite evidently perplexed, for Daphne had just phoned, asking him to break the news to me – with a warning that I might be emotionally distressed. No doubt he attributed my reaction to the *sang-froid* of the British aristocracy, accepting it thereafter as an example of how boys should behave.

After a period during which Henry convalesced out there in North Africa, came the surprise announcement that Daddy would be returning home to Britain. Everyone was in a flurry preparing for his arrival, perhaps even more so than I appreciated at the time. One point that took me by surprise was the way Mummy began again to rebuke me for knocking on her bedroom door before entering, proclaiming now that it was 'all too silly'. It made me wonder if she didn't recollect, as I did, that she herself had initially demanded that I do so.

The day came when Henry was actually back at Sturford with us, and we were all over him – treating him like a great war hero. It was only Val who didn't quite know how to react, since he couldn't really remember this man who had suddenly appeared at his bedside claiming to be his father. (He had promptly dived beneath the bedclothes, and it had proved difficult to persuade him to re-emerge.) We all vied to sit next to Daddy at table, to an extent that Mummy felt emotionally neglected, if not betrayed. I can remember Henry reassuring her that it was only a phase, and wouldn't last. But for quite some while, it did – for several years in fact.

The truth of the matter is that both Christopher and myself were just entering upon that psychological phase of development when identification with the father should be regarded as quite natural. We were both discovering what our maleness involved, and there wasn't much that Mummy could teach us about that. We watched Daddy, and tried to emulate his behaviour in all respects. And his words of commendation were what we each inwardly craved.

There was also this feeling that I wanted Daddy to feel that I was on his side. There was some vague uncertainty in my mind as to whether Daphne had been living her life in accordance with their marital rules. It wasn't an area where I could pose any direct questions, so I did the next best thing in trying to make a joke about it – more or less just to see if Henry laughed or took it to be no laughing matter. It must have been during his first week back at home with us, and we were serving ourselves to lunch from the sideboard in the dining-room. Without looking at him, I said: 'There are masses of new men for you to get to know, Dad.'

From the silence I learnt that the subject was as delicate as I'd feared. Then Daphne began protesting that this was untrue, and when we were next alone together she reproached me for saying things which could only make Daddy unhappy. Was that really the thought inside her head? I knew in my heart that there were relationships she wanted to keep hidden from his understanding. It evoked a memory of that occasion on the Araguaney when the nice man who had been playing with me suddenly became 'the nasty man' due to Henry's reappearance on the scene.

The honeymoon period in my relationship with Daddy didn't endure for very long. He announced quite curtly one day that it was time for disciplines to be reapplied. We seemed to have forgotten how to comport ourselves in public, and our table manners had gone to pieces. He wasn't troubled so much about Caroline, since he regarded her upbringing as a mother's responsibility, but as far as the boys were concerned he was going to make it his business to see that we shed all our recently-acquired bad habits and got back into the old way of doing things.

Nor was it just ourselves with whom he found fault. The garden which had been his pride before the war now showed signs of neglect. Mr Harris, the head gardener, was summoned to his study and fierce words were exchanged. The rumour lingered that it wasn't just on the subject of gardening. Mr Harris had managed to avoid enlistment in the armed services after failing his medical. But it was well known locally that he had been comforting the wives of certain servicemen who were now fighting up at the front. I know not what exactly may have been said when Henry dismissed Mr Harris, but I do know that the gardener rounded upon me when I crossed his path later that day, shouting abusive epithets at me for no apparent reason.

Although I didn't properly comprehend the situation at the time, Henry was reacting against the entire household with a reassertion of his dominance. He had learnt by now about all that had been going on in his absence, and there was a period perhaps when the marriage might have seemed to be on the rocks. But the two of them eventually managed to work out a *modus vivendi*, even if infidelities were now to be accepted on either side.

Some twenty years later I re-encountered [my mother's former lover]. He was more than a little well-wined at the time, and eager to converse with me on the subject of bygone days. He made me promise to tell my mother that she hadn't kept faith with him. He told me that he had only agreed to let her go back to my father if she promised that she would make the marriage work, and never to divorce him. In his inebriated mood he kept repeating that the subsequent divorce was tantamount to a deception of himself. But when I passed on his words to Daphne, she took them quite lightly.

Somewhere or other, deep down inside me, a potential schism had been opened up, so that I was looking in both parental directions, conscious of my roots and yet uncertain if they were truly cohesive. Essentially, my loyalties were still with Daphne. But there was a feeling in my mind that she was liable not to have any of the right answers – a lack of profundity, perhaps – and that she was a suspect vehicle for the emotional investment involved in any serious quest for my own identity.

> **Wan**ted, imp**or**tant, I'd been **flaun**ted and **vaun**ted to **heights**
> **un**en**light**ened, where your **love still** had **bright**ened
> the **nest** for this **fright-prone fledg**ling, **dodg**ing
> the **trunch**eoning **dog**mas of the **daddy**'s cur**mudge**only **jaws**.
> I was **your** ac**hieve**ment, and the **glory** had **glossed off**

125

in a **soft glow** on my **old pu**erile **shoul**ders.
It was **fold**ed into **ten**der **miss**ives from your **dis**tant **pres**ence,
di**gress**ed er**rat**ic from a **vib**rant **soc**ial **tribe**.
Im**bib**ing **glib un**der**stan**ding from your **shall**ow
**chal**ice, I'd **slurped** a **glut** of **good**ies to **nour**ish
my **flour**ishing **self**-es**teem**, **seem**ingly **bold**
and in**vul**nerable, **moul**ding a**bun**dant **zeal** for suc**cess**.
    How disconcerting then for me to find
    the trivial vanity within your mind.

# Chapter 16

## Worship: Burgeoning religious fervour

Religion was taken quite seriously at Ludgrove, predominantly in a Church of England, Protestant vein. There was a school chapel, with a different vicar or lay-preacher coming over to deliver us his sermon every Sunday morning. And Mr Barber did his own bit of preaching as well. He was concerned that we should all grow up as God-fearing citizens, and his attitude to life was indeed something that I was endeavouring to absorb.

There was only one voice from amongst our teachers which conveyed any different message, and that came from Cabbage Reed. He delighted in poking fun at some of the grosser absurdity in my developing Christian faith – like asking me if I thought my wings would have feathers when I was an angel up in Heaven.

'And what if I crept up behind you and tweaked one of them out?'

I knew that he liked me, and I knew that he never really intended that his question should be taken seriously. But it left me aware how there was a vein of disrespect in his own attitude towards what the rest of the masters at least pretended to revere.

Sometimes our faith was nurtured by particular dormitory monitors, who insisted that we kneel praying for the prescribed number of minutes. They were apt to give their own private sermons upon the rules of how to keep in with God, and some of their fervour inevitably washed off upon those under their control.

With such people to inspire me, I embarked upon a relatively brief period of religious fervour myself, believing that the world's salvation depended upon humans treating that subject a lot more seriously than they did at present. I remember taking a metal ring which had become detached from one of the chapel hassocks, and carrying it round with me as an amulet for my religious well-being. I even wrote a hymn or two, sending them back to Daphne for her own conversion. One of them began as follows.

> I love this world of good and ill,
> though evil through it stray,
> but God will make it good, he will,
> if we will just but pray.

The necessity for prayer was indeed the fundamental message that I wanted to put across to everybody. Indeed, I developed the idea almost to the point of obsession, which I inflicted upon the ears of my fellow supplicants to God at evening prayers, booming out the words of the Lord's Prayer and the Creed as if my salvation depended upon the sound of my communication reaching Heaven a few seconds in advance of that of the assembled throng. I only desisted from this piety, in fact, after Peter Munster (whom I so much admired) came over to me after evening prayers one day, and said: 'What do you think you are? A bloody fog-horn?'

I wasn't quite stopped in my tracks, however. After Henry had been wounded at El Alamein, I insisted upon Nanny's taking all of us children to the local church, just down the lane from Sturford, on several Sundays in succession. Nanny took it all with a bit of a giggle, without the faith that any good would come from our devotions. (One of her frequently quoted dictums was that God helps those who help themselves.) She couldn't get over the surprise on the Revd Mr Edmund's face when we all trooped in for the first time, for he had seen nothing of us since the departure of Miss Vigers.

My phase of religious intensity didn't endure for very long. Daddy was soon back home with us, relatively safe and sound. (The wound, incidentally, had been caused by a very small piece of shrapnel, which had lodged – until its removal under surgery – in his chest.) And if he didn't think that he required God's assistance to survive the war, then he was in a better position than myself to judge such matters. The tenor of his atheistic views, now reintroduced, was to mock those who took religion seriously, and because I very much wanted his approval and admiration, I subdued my fervour.

Or perhaps I should say that I bottled it up more secretly within myself.

# Chapter 17
## Sex: A homosexual awakening

It was also a question of switching from an interest in God to an increased interest in sex. So it is now time for me to recall how I had been evolving in that particular direction.

When I had first arrived at Ludgrove, a huge curiosity was aroused in me by discovering that a few of the boys had deformed cocks. My father had followed the upper-class fashion in having all of his sons circumcised, as indeed he himself had been. At Ludgrove, which was a distinctly aristocratic school, there were only a few uncircumcised cocks to perceive – or, to hazard a guess, I might say no more than one in ten. They were certainly an odd spectacle, as we all stood there queuing up for our baths.

There was one occasion when I took [Y], my best friend from Dorm 27, into the lavatory so that we could each examine more closely what this particular anatomical difference in the other entailed. But I judge that this only ranks as sexual curiosity, rather than as an instance of homosexual practice. And if it so happens that there was a potential affair between the two of us over that period, then it was eclipsed about a year later by his decision to drop me as a friend.

The message was originally conveyed to me during one of the school's Sunday walks, when we theoretically paired off with our best friends to traipse in a cluster vaguely around the master who was accompanying us. My particular friend kept accelerating, or decelerating, until I finally got the message that he didn't want to be paired with me. It was a wounding experience, but one that everyone needs to receive, sooner or later, and no matter from which sex.

In case this makes it sound as if I was becoming too puritanical over this period, then let me hastily interject some less savoury detail. My dog Charlotte got herself pregnant shortly after I went to Ludgrove – because of Miss Vigers' neglect (according to Nanny) or because of the attentions of the local farmer's dog, called Bubbles (according to others). Anyway, she produced seven puppies, who were a great delight to me during my first winter holidays back at Sturford.

I say 'a delight' because I do remember giving these puppies the tip of my penis to suck. I don't suppose that I did it very often, or even for very long, but it was a pleasure which I still recall. And I suppose that within any statistical enquiry I should now be listed amongst those who have indulged in bestial sex. I just mention it to keep the record straight.

In other matters I was learning how to behave correctly. Mr Barber was concerned to promote what might now be regarded as a male chauvinist attitude by which males were brought up to give gentlemanly deference to females, on principle – because it was self-evident that males ruled the world. But there was also this idea of modesty.

Prior to going to Ludgrove, I had displayed no inhibition about my naked body being viewed by other members of the family. But at Ludgrove I had learnt that it was more genteel to conceal my 'private parts' (as Mr Barber described them) from the eyes of ladies. I regarded my mother as one such lady, so on the first occasion when she walked into the nursery bathroom while I was sitting there in the bath, I hastily crossed my legs. Her reaction was one of irritation. ('Don't be so silly!', or some such remark.) I remember feeling confused as to whither the true direction of my education might lie.

That was the situation when dealing with ladies, of course. But there were other situations when I was dealing with females of a different kind. Up to the war there had always been a nurserymaid to assist Nanny in her tasks, and the convention continued until briefly after I had gone to school. The penultimate employee was a sexy little maid, who was probably no more than fifteen years of age. When I came home from school, she was up there in the nursery, and I was full of my own self-importance – being the one and only schoolboy, and all that. I dare say I did try to pose as Mr Big to her, but she certainly posed as Miss Sexy in response.

It was a matter of wrestling with her while she was seated in an armchair, if I remember correctly. I knew that there was something erotic in what we were doing – because the talk between us had been veering that way, if for no other reason. But in the process of wrestling with her, we were both aware how we were actually doing more than that – to the point when her hand slid between my legs and gave a furtive grasp to my genitals. Unfortunately, Nanny walked in at this moment. No one ever told me why this nurserymaid departed, but her mother came to collect her the very next morning. There was a silence over the whole issue which I felt safer not to question.

My sexual development over this period was really somewhat static. Our Vivian cousins had come to stay with us at one time, and the visit had been returned to the house where they now dwelt, near Ringwood in Hampshire. I was still very much aware of Sal's attractiveness, but we no longer felt quite so much at ease in one another's company. We were becoming self-conscious about the difference in gender, which entailed divergent paths towards maturity.

I was also a bit confused by some of the ideas Cal was now feeding to me with regard to my sexual identity. She imagined that I participated within a similar cultural environment to the one she herself experienced at Longstowe. For example, she was full of the notion that I ought to have a crush on someone. She told me the name of the girl upon whom she had affixed her own emotions, and demanded the fair exchange of my telling her who might be the object of my own. She didn't seem to understand that schoolboy cultures worked differently. I wasn't expected (when at Ludgrove) to have a crush upon anybody at all. But she continued to harass me on the subject until I pronounced that it must be [Z], who had at least served as a sort of elder-brother figure during the first terms. It was an incorrect analysis of my relationship with [Z], but Cal preferred to think that she had unearthed something crucial to an understanding of my soul.

The religious fervour phase was superseded by a burgeoning curiosity about sex. And this too stemmed from the influence of the particular dormitory monitor, who gave direction to what we all whispered about after the lights had been turned out. In Dorm 3 under [A], the emphasis was most definitely upon sex. We all pooled our knowledge on the subject, vying with one another to furnish more extensive detail than the others.

I had already been told about the facts of life by Caroline when I was seven years old, and I was now regarded as being relatively advanced in my education on such matters – by contemporary standards. But here in Dorm 3, I found that my authority was disputed, and by one of my new best friends. This was [B]. His version of the reproductory process was that it is milk, as opposed to urine, that the male injects into the woman – but it was into the tummy rather than into whatever women called their sex-things. (The most ingenious suggestion was that they might be called 'turkeys', in verbal contrast to cocks, and because they looked a bit like turkeys on a butcher's slab.) Anyway, I became marginally more confused than previously as to what exactly takes place at the conception of a child. Or perhaps [B] accepted my version of the procedure. I don't actually remember.

The conversations about sex went on deep into the night, [A], [B] and myself being the principal participants. And it gradually took a more active turn. [A] told us how there was a boy from Hastings that he knew in the holidays, who had shown him how you could produce that milk-like stuff from which babies are made. All you had to do was to pull the skin on your cock rapidly up and down until it squirted out. So all three of us lay there, trying our damnedest to achieve that result – without any success, I might add. But the sensation was certainly pleasant, and we encouraged each other with a certain manual assistance.

So thus it was that I learnt how to masturbate. And now that I knew, I taught it to others. There was [C], to whom I demonstrated what need-ed to be done while we were isolated up in the sick room that term, suffering from flu. It all helped to pass the hours of a dreary illness, which became enjoyable as a result, once we were recuperating. The only problem is that whenever I meet [C] in adult life, he is always liable to greet me with the public pronouncement: 'Why, there's the man who taught me how to masturbate!'

And there was [D]. In his case the tuition was delivered in the school latrines. And he shocked me greatly – by peeing (as I then supposed) up my arm while I was milking him. I simply didn't believe him when he said he couldn't help it. Only much later, once I too had mastered the art of orgasm, did I appreciate that this, in all probability, is what had then occurred.

# Chapter 18

## Authority: Learning to control others

Going to boarding school had furnished me with the initial opportunity for reacting with my peer group to discover who was dominant over another. The classroom was less of a crucial arena than the dormitories. And at Ludgrove, 'the earlybedders' filled three special dormitories, and followed a time schedule different from that of the older boys.

There were about five of us new kids during my first term in Dorm 27, alongside the dormitory monitor. In that the latter only joined us at a later hour, for much of the time we had to work out our own rules for interplay. Invariably, there was one individual more than the next who was apt to suggest such rules, or even to be left in charge of a situation by Matron, or her assistants.

It was some advantage having an elder brother, in that his authority could be evoked in the event of a dispute. And there was always Munster, whom I regarded somewhat in that vein, although I was never quite sure if he would really back me up if we all appealed to his better judgement. Morrison on the other hand quite genuinely possessed an elder brother. So he initially dominated our group. But I was much concerned on this issue of wanting to see that my rules, rather than someone else's, were those that were adopted. And during my second term – in Dorm 28 this time, and in different company – I prided myself on the idea that I was perhaps dominant.

It was also a question of seeing that the new kids knew their place, in relation to those who had been at the school for longer. They must learn not to be cheeky – a matter that would be corrected by physical chastisement if the offence were repeated too often. But there was also a taboo against the idea of bullying. All of these matters required a delicate assessment of what should be judged permissible, and what discouraged. There was also the whole pecking order to consider. And I learnt as quickly as the next person whom it was that I might be entitled to peck, and whose authority should be accepted without demur.

Then came the question of who was dominant at Sturford, within the home environment. I never disputed Cal's authority. Our original training on the question of hierarchy was too strong for me. Nor did I ever feel any challenge to me from either of my younger brothers on that score. But while Daddy was away there in the Middle East, there was a general loss of control over what took place at home – due largely to the war situation. We weren't quite as much as before the masters in our own home.

There were the evacuees, for example. The crippled children hadn't stayed with us for very long, but the authorities soon lodged with us the [E] family, who came from London's East End. I was at Ludgrove when they first arrived, only discovering that all was not well from Nan and Chris when I returned home for the holidays. Chris informed me how these children had laughed at his discomfiture when he took a step backwards to end up with a foot in the pond – on his first sight of them playing in the same garden as himself. And Nanny was full of tales about their territorial infringement, causing her to shout at them frequently from the nursery window forbidding them to trespass.

The situation became notably worse after Nanny had taken on the eldest of the [E] children to come and do the washing-up in the nursery. It had been an experiment without any chance of success. Coming from where they did, they knew next to nothing of the feudal culture that existed deep in the heart of Wessex, and the whole idea of domestic service was utterly foreign to their natures. And when it came to Nanny's laying down the law on behalf of this family who seemed to think they were so much above everyone else, then young Miss [E] wasn't going to stand for it. She endured the job for less than a week, and then never appeared again. Indeed, this was the last occasion that Nan had any young girl to work for her, so the desertion rankled deeply. Thereafter, for the most part, she had to perform such menial tasks herself.

I daresay that Miss [E] was about fifteen – a biggish young woman – and her three sisters were some years younger, perhaps around eight, nine and ten. What irritated greatly from our own point of view was the way in which these evacuees seemed to be poking fun at us upon our own territory. The younger ones would stick their faces under the macrocarpa hedge, which separated the front garden from the kitchen entrance to Sturford, making faces at us while Chris and I were riding our bicycles upon the lawn. We made the occasional bicycle charge in their direction, to drive them away. But they regarded the hedge as the demarcation of their own bastion, and after retreating, they would invariably return, as aggressively cheeky as ever.

Well, the day arrived when we were feeling more pugnacious than usual. The Gilmour family was visiting, and Sandy (who was about two years older than me) was surprised that we let them get away with such cheek. So in an atmosphere of showing off to one another we were soon involved in a hue and cry, racing round on our bicycles to cut off their retreat from under the macrocarpa hedge. They ran screaming – and it was now our turn to jeer.

If we had left the matter rest there, it would have counted as a great success. Unfortunately, in the full flush of victory we pressed forward, abandoning our bicycles and chasing them on foot until they took refuge behind the door into the basement, where their own quarters were situated. This they bolted in our faces, and we stood there clamouring for their blood on the outside – with no specific idea in mind as to what we should do if we got hold of them. But it came as a big surprise to all of us when the door suddenly opened, and there stood Miss [E], totally unabashed by our numbers, and demanding to know what it was that we wanted.

She neatly side-tracked the issue of whether or not her sisters had the right to make faces at us from under the macrocarpa hedge by suggesting that our problem was that we seemed to think we were better than they. We were thus enticed into making our stand on that issue, jeering at them for being 'just girls'. Miss [E] declared boldly that she was quite prepared to have a fight with us, if that was what we wanted – which of course we didn't. She was certainly bigger than any of the males I had fought, and fighting a girl (even if I turned out to be stronger) wasn't really a situation that might bring any credit to us. So we felt obliged to withdraw, after flinging a few more bravado taunts in her direction.

But there was now a distinct antipathy between the two families, and there seemed so little that we could do about it, to persuade them to seek their accommodation elsewhere. I thought that this was a situation where I had the rest of my family fully in my support. So when I caught a rat in the garden, after killing it, I shoved it down through the grill through which the [E] family received their light and their ventilation of air. And some days after performing this feat, I boasted to Daphne about what I had done, suggesting that the smell of the decaying rat must surely precipitate their departure.

I was now quite alarmed to discover that she felt I had overstepped the bounds of fair play. Or, in any case, that I ought to have judged that if the [E] family caught the plague (or whatever it is that one might catch from dead rats), the infection might then spread to our own family. No, on the grounds of good sanitation, I would have to go down into the basement and retrieve the rotting corpse from their ventilation shaft – a performance that cost me acute embarrassment, even though I was accompanied by Mr Harris, the head gardener, to give me moral support (although I dare say his true sympathies were on the other side).

In its way, however, the protest was effective in that the [E] family did depart quite soon afterwards. And Daphne was more careful thenceforward to refrain from such public-spirited war effort in offering any portion of Sturford for the use of displaced persons. Not that this left us problem-free, since it was always difficult to find enough staff to run the place. And we did have some experience of the kind of person who got sent to us from the reserve pool of labour at the work exchange.

One who arrived to fill the post of butler looked at first sight almost ideal for the job, possessing a set of butler's clothes that convinced us that his tales of wide experience in this profession must be genuine. But there were also rumours that he had suffered from mental illness, which might explain why he wasn't being required to contribute more valuably towards the war effort. And our conviction that this might be the explanation increased as the days went by. His reminiscences of service in aristocratic homes proliferated until they reached a point when Daphne at least knew that he was telling fibs. And she felt alarmed to the extent of discomfort when he insisted on rushing up to give a tug downwards at her skirt, so that it wouldn't have a crease when she sat down at the dining-room table.

My own experience of his oddity occurred when he came to sit with me and Chris beside the pond on a sunny day. One of the crazes at Ludgrove had been to ignite a newspaper by focusing the sun's rays through a magnifying glass, and naturally enough, I had also felt the pain that it could cause on my naked hand. So trying to be funny, I suppose, I applied the rays of the magnifying glass to his hand, outstretched on the grass and unsuspecting, while he was feeding us with more of his bogus stories about those capers with the nobility.

I was taken quite by surprise in that he didn't take it as a mild practical joke, but leapt up with a cry of anguish, or pain, and started pursuing me round the lawn, having grabbed the magnifying glass from my hand, demonically intent upon some tit-for-tat operation. It was just a case of over-reaction, I dare say. Yet it struck all of us that he wasn't the same type of person that we'd employed in the days before the war disrupted everything.

We had another problem too, in that during the days gone by it had been Daddy rather than Mummy who would have dealt with any such dismissal. And this particular individual was quite charismatic, in his own sort of way. Not for the first time, Daphne flinched from such a task. So Mr Gill was left to perform the dishonour, during one of our family outings up to London. The butler had vacated the premises by the time we returned home – although Daphne did get sent some letters lamenting that he had never before been so disgracefully treated by members of the British aristocracy.

# Chapter 19

## Activities: Filling out the length of the day

I do not think that we were adventurous children. We had a safe home environment, with routines that were fulfilled in a spirit of boredom. But we never enthused about what we were doing, nor sought greatly to enrich the day's eventless schedule.

I think it does need to be stated in this context that our parents never paid any special interest in our adolescent development. We were being raised in a spirit of egocentricity, which increased rather than diminished after Henry's return from North Africa. Both parents then had plenty of their own problems to contend with, and not much heed was given to whether we might be developing any particular ones of our own. By and large, however, at that point in time we were not doing so, for we were reasonably contented, each of us in his own self-centred way of life.

But I'll try to furnish a more extensive sketch of the kind of activities that kept me occupied over this period.

I learnt to play draughts, and then graduated to chess quite early while I was at Ludgrove. I was good at both, but there wasn't much interest shown in the game after I had been there a few terms. I never really caught on to the habit of reading novels, incidentally, mainly because my reading speed didn't quite match those who were at the same level as me in the school.

Back at Sturford during the holidays, in the malaise of general boredom, all too often there was a feeling of not knowing what to do with ourselves next.

Whenever we were left to our own devices (as, indeed, was nearly always the case) we remained uninspired as to how best to use such independence. There was a brief period when we became enthused in the construction of a private 'den' in the garden. But even this was an idea lifted from the Cobbold and Crawley families, whom we sometimes used to visit at their grandmother's home of Clarendon Park, near Salisbury.

Anyway, we constructed our own den, and I dug a pit in front of the sole entry, which I camouflaged brilliantly with sticks and grass, to discourage adult intrusion. Unfortunately, the only adult that we caught was Nanny, who came storming out in a rage one day because we were so late for lunch, falling into the bear trap before heeding our shrill cries of warning. It was a mirthful situation, to which both Chris and myself gave way – not that it was appreciated by Nanny, even though she emerged from the ordeal without any broken bones.

Henry was irked, on his return from Africa, at the way 'the boys' now went slouching round the place with hands thrust deep within our pockets. He criticised us for 'lacking the gumption' to find things to do. He also remarked that we seemed to take after Daphne, whom he categorised as a town lady, in that we had no real addiction to country life. And by this he was really getting at my comparative disinterest in the gamekeeper activities which had so much enthused himself as a boy.

My enthusiasm for rabbiting had indeed waned greatly, although Chris and I did sometimes go out with Tom Renyard for one thing or another. After my tenth birthday, however, he was teaching me to shoot rabbits with his small four-ten shotgun, and that greatly revived my interest in blood sports. But I experienced all the emotional indecision it created in my own mind as to whether to give way to the hunter's joy at a kill, or to the remorse that seemed equally natural to someone who had thus caused the sudden (and unnecessary) extinction of life in some animal or bird that, a few seconds previously, had been a delight to watch.

Yet the killer phase in me was waxing, and for my eleventh birthday present my parents gave me a Holland & Holland sixteen-bore shotgun. For the remainder of my schooldays I repressed all questions as to whether I ought to be indulging in such sports, and merely attempted to emulate the sort of person that Henry would admire the most – which entailed trying to shoot better (and more blood-thirstily) than any of my contemporaries.

I was in fact presented with this gun at the Christmas prior to my eleventh birthday, when Daphne was busy entertaining at Sturford a bunch of officers which included Rex Whistler, the artist. There was a heavy snowfall that January, and I can remember the pleasure he gave us children in coming out to join in our snowball fights. And his method of thanking Daphne for all the hospitality she had been furnishing for him was to paint my portrait. (It was one of the last paintings he ever did, since he was killed in action soon after the invasion of Normandy.) But he painted me with sixteen-bore shotgun in hand, in what might now be regarded as a somewhat untypical pose.

Rex spent much of his time at Sturford with us in the schoolroom, demonstrating his artistic talent in a variety of ways. He showed us how to draw a face which, when turned upside down, was a completely different face – almost so that you no longer perceived the original one if viewed the other way up. And he did scribble-drawings for us too. He would ask one of us to draw a few lines at random, but not just round and round in overlapping circles, and he would then work on these to produce highly animated sketches – usually of eccentric people with or without animal accompaniment.

This approach to drawing has remained with me to the present day. By that I mean the imprecision of detail that any scribble might initiate, combined with the perception of opportunity, and the chance potential that lurks within any grouping of random lines. It nudged me in the direction of expressionism in art, which Rex himself might have found curious, if he had lived, for his own painting style was hardly to be associated with that particular school.

Artistic talent never proved to be much of an advantage at Ludgrove, for the school's activities were definitely oriented towards sport, and I remained very average indeed in those fields of enterprise. I enjoyed my cricket better than I did my soccer, where I never did manage to obtain an adequate control of the ball with my feet. But there were also courts for playing squash, and Eton fives, and I did manage to be better than average at the latter. Also at boxing, where I remained constantly amongst those in the running to win all the competitions. I was somehow always better at performing proficiently with my hands, as opposed to my feet, but such proficiency diminished once a bat or racket was introduced between my hand and the ball.

One of my principal rivals in the boxing ring was [X], who was just a bit older and heavier than me. In any case, his punch was definitely more solid, and contrasted with my own more stylish tactic of frequently stabbing with left jabs to the face. On the two occasions when we both reached the finals in the same competition, he in fact emerged as the winner on points, but they were regarded as excellent fights by the sergeant-major who instructed us. And it was our rivalry in this field which brought us together for a while in close friendship – combined with scholastic rivalry over the same period for the top place in Cabbage Reed's division.

We became constant companions over a period of about a year, and it was Cabbage who dubbed us with the affectionate nicknames of Romeo and Juliet. There was nothing overtly homosexual in the relationship, but it was a friendship that had all the traditional bonding of boarding-school mutual admiration. The fact that I was deemed to be Juliet (to his Romeo) galled me a bit, but I feel obliged to admit that it would have been ridiculous to have identified us the other way round – if such was the duo after which we had to be named.

My spell of scholastic interest diminished greatly when I rose to the next division, under a different teacher. And this coincided with my emergence, in image, as one of the school's daredevils.

This had all started in [A]'s dormitory, where the habit of night-prowling (amongst other things) was encouraged. The kudos was really in the presentation of ourselves as boys who thus demonstrated that we were prepared to risk a 'swishing' through this defiance of authority. Those of us who indulged in such (totally unnecessary and unamusing) activities were, by these acts of daring, mutually encouraged to regard themselves as future commando or SAS recruits. And in the sphere of macho development, this was of course not quite so trivial an ambition as it might otherwise sound to be.

Mr Barber, however, was keeping track of such undesired development, increasing his patrols of the dormitory area and inflicting the expected swishing upon those who were caught in the act. My friend [B] got caught (and swished), and for one reason or another, Alan ('Ali') Barber appeared to know exactly whom the as yet unswished night-prowlers might be. I was never in fact caught, and never in fact swished while I was at preparatory school – but he was certainly contemplating such a remedy for me over this period. When [X], who had been given four strokes for some other reason which I don't recall, showed me the bright blue and red weals on his bum, I felt quite nervous about the prospect of such a punishment inflicted by Ali's hand.

Eventually there was a confrontation of sorts – over mistaken suspicions. I had been standing with a ball of plasticine in my hand, and I was going to see if it stuck against the wall on flinging it there with some force. But just as I was almost in motion to perform this act, in walked Ali – who seemed convinced that I had been intent on breaking a window, or something of the kind. So he insisted that I continue in my intent, with himself present. I did as he bade, although he remained far from convinced that I was engaged upon such a trivial pursuit as trying to stick a piece of plasticine by impact upon the wall, especially when such a feat proved impossible. But it was happier for me in getting arrested (so to speak) for such a trivial misdemeanour, which then triggered the homily he had prepared for me in the event of a swishing.

He talked to me actually in sensible vein, questioning the rewards and pleasures from such activities as night-prowling. Wouldn't it be of more value to myself to enjoy the refreshment of a good night's sleep? And what was the purpose in striving to be a daredevil when in reality I was quite well-behaved? Although not all at once, the logic sank home, and thereafter (for some while at least) I desisted from putting such emphasis upon the need to rebel against authority.

# PART FOUR

# LUDGROVE (2)

# Chapter 20

## Siblings: A realignment

After the experience of Miss Vigers, my parents decided that it probably wasn't necessary to employ another governess. Not that Christopher's scholastic performance at the Lord Weymouth School had furnished evidence of a better education to be obtained there. He still had problems in that area, now that he had moved on to Ludgrove. But there were two of our cousins, Charlie Wilson and Nick Vivian, who had come to stay at Sturford during the term-time so that they also could attend the Lord Weymouth – and the latter had fared distinctly worse.

Nick was very young at the time, and I dare say that he had been upsetting his peer group by boasting about his Thynne family connection. But this still seems inadequate as an explanation for the fact that one of their schoolmasters found him suspended by his arms from a tree in the school grounds, after he had failed to reappear in the classroom after the morning break.

No, it was decided it might be safest not to send Valentine to the Lord Weymouth, prior to his moving on to Ludgrove. Nanny persuaded Daphne that he might receive more kindly treatment if he went to the Lord Weymouth's rival private school in Warminster – Saint Monica's, which was run exclusively by nuns. Both Nan and Val were in any case perfectly satisfied with the arrangement.

There was a curious realignment taking place around this time, Chris spending far more of his time with Val during our holidays from school. I had probably been too bossy as an elder brother during our previous relationship, and it was quite natural for Chris to move in the direction of bossing someone younger instead, for a change, rather than being constantly on the receiving end. So as far as boyish games were concerned, I now began to find myself increasingly without fraternal companions.

Now that we were seeing a lot more of Henry, who had been posted as an instructor at Bovington in Dorset, a rivalry was developing between Chris and myself to win esteem in his eyes. We were both at the age when a father's regard acquires great importance. The whole of our Western culture is geared that way, and it was certainly how we were brought up at Ludgrove – to emulate the father figure in all his ideas, and even in his mannerisms. I had a good try at doing this, as best I knew how, for I wanted nothing better than to assist him in whatever chore he might be doing.

> **Hold**ing my **pink face** like a **mir**ror to your **gaze**,
> I **braz**enly **stretch**ed a **wretch**ed **arm** to **palm**
> your **treas**ured **bless**ing of **proud** paternal re**gard**,
> **plac**ing the **prize** in **star-span**gled **eyes**.
> **Siz**ing your **foot**prints with a **puppy**'s **glut**inous **pads**,
> I **gladly straddl**ed my **own meag**re **shad**ow,
> **plod**ding your ex**cit**ing **wake**, with **rak**ish **ges**tures
> fashionably **flaun**ting a **braggart**'s **swagger-stick**.
> **Pick**ing the **tall flow**ers with the **sour fruit**,
> I **beaut**ifully **loot**ed the **brash treas**ure from the **pleas**ure
> **gard**en of **aris**tocratic re**nown**, **clown**ing
> to your **whim**sy with **par**donable **grim**ly **seri**ous intent.
> No criticism then could touch my mind,
> for you were everything – and I was blind.

What astounded me was that Chris should emerge as rather better than myself at winning his esteem. Nothing in my life up to this point had prepared me for such an outcome. I knew that Daphne held me in higher regard, and so had Miss Vigers. If Nan felt a secret preference for Chris, her attitude was outwardly well balanced. And when it came to our performance at Ludgrove, there was no question about my end of term reports being better than those of my younger brother, who had caused some anxiety to both parents and teachers alike with his evident disinterest in education. When it came to athletic ability, we were roughly on a par, except at boxing. Not that we ever fought over this period, but my pre-eminence in that field (combined with my age advantage) always demanded a certain deference to my ultimate demands. So how can I explain that Henry came to prefer Chris to myself, when all the advantages might seem to have been ranged on my side?

I shall venture some manner of explanation.

There was at least one occasion when Henry overheard me telling Chris what he should be doing, with unnecessary authoritarian stress. The time I particularly remember occurred just outside his study, and it could well be that I was behaving in this fashion especially so that Daddy would perceive just how dominant (and superior) I really was. But he called me into his study for a few friendly words of rebuke, telling me that I had too high an opinion of myself – that I ought to put more effort into thinking about what others might want.

There were some letters too when he accused me of 'selfishness'. It occurs to me now that what he really meant may have been egocentricity. But this was never one of the terms that he employed.

My own comment on this subject is that the way in which we were being raised encouraged such egocentricity to develop. Our parents weren't particularly interested in our day-to-day development. It might even be said that they were happy provided that we didn't become intrusive within their own lives. I don't think Henry should have been surprised if egocentricity became a characteristic of such upbringing, even if the question remains open as to why I should have developed more egocentrically than my other siblings. But the answer there, of course, is that I was developing an isolation from the rest of the brood, in the direction already indicated.

Perhaps the greatest insight that I can offer on how I might have seemed objectionable in some people's eyes comes in a letter that I wrote to Henry, who was then back in action again. (More on that later.) I was writing to him about an outing with a pony called Topsey, which had been loaned to us by the Jolliffe family at Amerdown. A note is discernible of almost savage competitiveness in spirit with my two brothers, and especially with Chris, marking a determination on my side perhaps to be perceived by Henry as the most laudable of his sons. But on reading this letter, I am left with the uncomfortable feeling that there might well have been substance to the judgement that Chris was then a more amiable creature than myself. It reads as follows.

> In the trap she is lovely, but in actual riding I am not so sure that she is. More than likely it is my bad riding, but Chris, who is thought to be better than me, got on very badly too. First of all I offered to lead the pony while Val rode it. He got on but kept on saying to Nan: 'Nanny, I do not feel all that safe!' Nan went on saying: 'It'll be all right dear!' But

Topsey decided she didn't want to go out, and began to trot back to the stables across the front lawn. As I could not stop her to begin with, Val began to scream, so Nan rushed up to take him off.

Then I got on, trying to look very grand but feeling very small. All went well until I had to pass a wasp's nest. I put her into a fast trot, but could not pull her out of it. So Chris came to the rescue and we stopped her. Then I (very kindly!) said that he could have a ride. To begin with he did jolly well, so I hurriedly said: 'I think it's my turn now!'

This time I did much better. In fact I reached the head-keeper's lodge without mishap.

When we were about to start back, I had my first victory over Chris. He said I could have his turn if I liked. I felt jolly cocky, and I still do. He probably would have deceived some people, but not ME!!!

I was getting on fine till I suddenly remembered that hill by St Mary's church. I also remembered that it was very steep, so I again told Chris that I thought it was his turn. But when I tried to dismount, Topsey refused to stop. So Chris had to come to my rescue for the second time. I felt very annoyed.

When he got into the saddle, to my joy, Topsey went off and he could not stop her. In fact he asked me in the end to take her by the bridle and lead her down the hill. I did so willingly, as you can well imagine. I think I had the best of that ride anyway. This time I do not think that younger brother has beaten elder brother, as he often does.

So much for the letter. But there may have been more to my father's disapproval of me than just that particular slant on my personality. Perhaps it is relevant to talk about the family stamp album. Under the influence of Miss Vigers I had once been a keen collector of stamps. This was shortly before Henry embarked for the Middle East when, almost as a leaving present, he donated to me the family stamp album which had been compiled over the best part of a century by both my grandfather, Thomas, and by Henry in his turn. So I was now regarded as being old enough to participate within the family tradition and make my own contribution to the collection. And I began by being very keen to do so.

While he was away in Africa, however, I did not see fit to take my stamp album to Ludgrove with me. Quite frankly, it would have been unwise of me if I had because, even within a school for the sons of the relatively rich, there were thieving fingers, and this album did contain some valuable old stamps that had been collected by my grandfather during the previous century. For this reason I am still offended that Henry, after his return to this country, should have felt that I was slighting his gift to me by my established habit of leaving the album at home, rather than taking it back to school with me. He wrote and told me that since I evidently didn't appreciate the album, he was taking it away from me and giving it to Christopher instead.

Now this small act was typical of Henry. Whatever he gave, he felt that he had the right to take back – from which we might infer that his children had no rights of property such as is customary to suppose within Western culture. It also coincided with the development of his authoritarian, dictatorial streak of which I shall be writing at some length later on.

At this point however, I merely wish to emphasise that he took the album away from me, and gave it to Chris, who was of course very careful to take it back to Ludgrove with him for the first few terms. But when he too eventually saw the wisdom of leaving it back at home, Henry had no objections to offer.

To offer an explanation for Henry's preference from another angle, we should remember that he himself had once been the underprivileged and intellectually backward younger son. He perhaps found it easier to identify with Christopher's problems rather than with my own. And when he overheard me speaking in an overbearing manner to Chris, he was quick to sympathise with the underdog because it paralleled his own experience at Longleat prior to his emergence as the only surviving male heir – and perhaps even after then, inasmuch that his two eldest sisters were always inclined to assert themselves, at his expense.

I was mystified more than troubled, at this stage in my life by Henry's attitude towards myself. I had the feeling that he must be missing out on some essential piece of information which I might readily be able to furnish. After all, I had established such an excellent filial relationship with my headmaster at Ludgrove. I could not understand why it should be difficult to acquaint my real father with that excellence, so that I might quickly emerge as his favourite son.

But I was also beginning to take note of the areas where Chris was beginning to score his successes – in whatever field.

And there was an occasion when Cal got hold of a paperback entitled *Meet Yourself as You Really Are.* This was a book where you were enabled to slot yourself within different stereotypes for personality, in accordance with particular psychological theories – like the distinction between extroverts and introverts, manics and depressives, or between schizoids and paranoids. We all enthused upon the task of unearthing our inner selves, with conviction offered for all that we read. But I felt greatly peeved afterwards, when we arrived at the point where Christopher's personality was to be exposed to public view, to be told that of all the characters categorised in this book, his was the best, whereas in its analysis of my own, I had been served out with a whole gamut of psychoses and depressions – which promptly accumulated on thus learning how I had been described.

I believed implicitly in the authenticity of this book, but I simply couldn't swallow that Chris had a better character than myself. So I felt indignant in my conviction that he must have been cheating by offering false information to the list of questions that had been supplied, and I rounded on him critically on that issue.

His friend Nick Cobbold had found himself with the identical character assessment, so I maintained that this was proof they were acting in unison to acquire our admiration on false premises. But I was then trounced by Mrs Cobbold (the mother) who took their side to say how accurate she felt the assessments really were, with regard to each of our personalities. So I felt saddled with the book's conclusions.

My one let-out was to convince myself that if they had characters which were good, mine might still be the more interestingly complex. I settled for that.

But I was becoming increasingly aware how Chris was now striving to better my performance generally all round – apart from in scholastic ability, for he seemed to have turned his interest away from education completely. Yet there were other areas in which his constant challenge was made known to me. In music, for example, there was no doubt that at Ludgrove I was regarded to have superior talent. Here at Sturford, though. Chris acquired a certain proficiency on the mouth-organ, and the tonette, which was the plastic imitation of a recorder. He played these frequently, over a brief spell, until he had received Henry's commendation on being a better musician than myself – a judgement with which I didn't concur. It made me wonder why he never bothered to check up with our teachers as to which was the more musically gifted. But it was his commendation that we both so desperately wanted to win.

Also in the field of art, Chris spent much of his holiday time over one period studiously copying Walt Disney caricatures. But what irritated me in particular was the way in which he then presented them as his own original drawings. When I accused him of copying them, he firmly denied it – until I set down the book from which they had been copied in front of him. Yet once again, others were not being so critical as to where the originals were to be found. And on this occasion it was not only Henry but also the lady who taught us drawing at Ludgrove who began praising his artistic talent in contrast to my own. As I saw it, Chris was fraudulent – and knew it. But Henry didn't seem to judge things that way. And in Christopher's favour, I must record that the art teacher at Ludgrove held just as high an esteem for his talent as for my own.

There was also the glimmering of a sexual rivalry emerging. I had been much smitten by the beauty of my cousin Sally-Anne – as previously related. And there were still occasions when we exchanged visits. But I was now feeling increasingly inhibited about the whole subject of how a young boy should communicate with a young girl. It was certainly not a subject that had been covered within the school curriculum, and there were more 'Thou shalt not' injunctions than suggestions of permissibility in anything that I had recently learnt. It seemed only natural that I should keep my distance.

But Chris was made of different metal, appearing to be unaffected by such inhibitions. His behaviour towards Sal might even have been described as mildly flirtatious, which disconcerted me greatly – as if it were a question of his not having to abide by the rules of the game. It had surely been long established that Sal was my girl-friend and not his, but I was conscious of a taboo against even discussing the matter with him openly. So he continued to flirt with Sal, and although I didn't identify my feelings as such at the time, I was jealous.

That this was no freak situation became evident to me at a children's dance that was held at Claridges around this time. Both Chris and I had been seated at the tea-table which included Princess Alexandra, and it must have been faintly in the minds of those who were organising this event that I might eventually emerge as an utterly suitable candidate for her hand in marriage. (For this was long prior to my development in what they would regard as a mistaken direction.) But it was Chris rather than myself who had the audacity to keep dancing with her, and I was much aware how adults, like Nanny, were commenting upon this – somehow as if he had put my own nose out of joint.

If there were areas for potential future discord with Chris becoming established over this period, there was little for immediate concern. It was only natural that he should be striving to emerge with an identity of his own, and by challenging my own established superiority in certain fields he was managing to do just that. But there was little hostility in the relationship, and we really didn't fight with one another. In fact there was remarkably little friction between all of us children in general.

There was no need to be any with Val, who was still the baby of the family and still spoilt by Nan, since he didn't exactly represent any challenge to the state of our individual egos. Perhaps the most revealing insight into our personal relationship might be furnished by quoting once again from the letter cited previously.

> Valentine comes down to me in the mornings to learn what all the butterflies and moths in my collection are called. If I have any spare ones, I give them to him when he can remember their names. It gives me a lot of authority over him. If he's a nuisance, I only have to say: 'All right, give me back those butterflies!' And he immediately turns into an angel, willing to do whatever I might want him to do.

The impermanence of gifts was an attitude which Henry had fed to me, of course, and which Val accepted as much as the rest of us. But we all liked Val. Within his good nature we discerned an odd combination of squealing malleability and stubborn obstinacy – often depending upon whether Nanny was standing within earshot. Her instant support was always his surest defence, but if she wasn't in the vicinity, then he was quite capable of holding out, incommunicado, against whatever threat we might present to him.

Collectively, we must have created something of a domineering family background for the little boy. I can remember one occasion when the three brothers were all sharing a room in a London hotel. Chris and I were awoken by the vocal strains of Val, lying there fast asleep while lying stiffly to attention in his bed, and singing *God Save The King* at the top of his lungs. I suppose we did exert that kind of influence over him.

Even more than myself, Val displayed a naive gullibility which made him an appropriate butt for Henry's bouts of teasing.

There was the joke about prehistoric gorilla-men living in our woods. When we were all accompanying Henry on his inspections of the forestry, he would pretend to espy one of these creatures lurking somewhere in the undergrowth behind us. His pace would quicken, and he would begin to simulate a general state of alarm. By the time Chris and I were joining him in this pretence, finally making a dash for the unexplained security of some distant clump, Val was invariably bounding after us in screaming terror. But he was enjoying that terror, only half-believing it to have foundation in reality. And there were many occasions when he would prompt a repetition of the performance by enquiring hopefully if there were any gorillamen in the particular stretch of woods that we might then be crossing.

Turning to my relationship with Cal, it wasn't growing any closer. I loved her as dearly as ever, but there could be no getting away from the fact that we were being brought up as different species of human being, myself male against her female. There seemed to be little overlap within our expectations from life. And the methods of persuasion were utterly different. Soon after his return from Africa, Henry pronounced that it was the three boys that he was going to make it his business to take in hand, mending the errors in their ways by whatever disciplines he found necessary. Caroline was to remain Daphne's concern.

I think it may be true to say that Cal was also emerging as Daphne's favourite over this period. She had the unique status of being the only girl, whereas the rest of us were lumped together into a common identity, and generally referred to as 'the boys'. Daphne shared confidences with Cal which she would no longer have seen fit to share with me – like the identity of the lover who had perhaps meant the most to her: Nigel Grahame, as I was to be informed much later. I never appreciated at the time how he had been something very special to Mummy, although we inherited his giant poodle called Chocolate after he had been killed in action. Daphne and Cal were growing close together as female confidantes, whereas I was beginning to perceive that my own identity rested somewhere firmly upon the other side of the gender fence.

There is also evidence within a letter I wrote home from Ludgrove that I was feeling under pressure from Cal to submit to her determination of my identity in directions other than I might choose for myself. I was in the sick room at the time, as one of the numerous victims of a flu epidemic. I wrote as follows.

> Last night I had a horrible nightmare. I dreamt that I lived
> in a very small cottage haunted by Caroline. For some rea-
> son I kept on fishing sixpenny pieces from my pockets,

while an invisible Cal snatched them away from me on each occasion. Then I found myself outside, with knives being thrown at me. Then I was inside again, playing planchette with some strangers. And it was the ghost of Cal who was sending messages to us. She wanted us to burn down the house. So we did this, and I woke up sweating all over, with a high fever ...

The interpretation (as I now see it) furnishes a picture of me attempting, in vain, to establish my own identity and worth, and Cal obstructing me in that endeavour. It is also clear that I fear the prospect of persecution from the world outside if I am to be deprived of the protection of my relationship with her. But she seems determined that I shall find no other. It should also be noted that the value that I was trying to set on my own identity was a strictly modest one – a mere sixpence, which was very nearly the smallest silver coin. Perhaps I wasn't being so humble as to suggest that my identity should be represented by a copper coin, but I had no grandiose illusions about myself as worth a florin or half a crown, let alone a sovereign, of course. I am stressing this because the general line of Henry's criticism of me at that time was that I was 'too big for my boots,' and needed 'to be cut down to size.'

It strikes me nowadays that Cal took me very much for granted as a person, and that she never appreciated how loving, and indeed how deferential, I had always been towards her. It was a one-sided love affair, and she never particularly noted the areas where I was in fact quite gifted. I think she wanted to see herself as supreme – if only she had been a boy. So even my boyish talents were downgraded in her judgement.

By way of an example, I might indicate my physical strength. Never in my life had I assaulted Cal, with a view to letting her see that I was tougher in combat than herself – despite all my established prowess in the boxing ring. Where my sister was concerned, everything was verbal in whatever antagonisms that might arise between the two of us. Then Cal went to stay for a brief while with our Vivian cousins, and she encountered a very different kind of fraternal relationship between Sal and Nick. There was a similar age-gap between them as between ourselves, but young Nicholas would hurl himself in fury at his elder sister so that she found it difficult to control him. And it was on witnessing such an onslaught that Cal lent her backing to Sal, and received the full force of an angry young male in counterattack.

On returning to Sturford, she told me how she had suppressed Nick with some difficulty, but that he was far stronger than I. When this little titch finally reached Ludgrove, and even if we had been of similar age, there is no doubt at all that he would have been wiped off the floor by me in any boxing contest, or any other contest of strength. He never acquired any prestige at school as a pugilist. So it galled me greatly to hear Cal assessing our relative physical strength in this fashion. And what galled me even more was her insistence that we have our own trial of strength, right there in her bedroom – all perfectly friendly, but she wanted to see which of the two of us was really the stronger!

The truth of the matter (as I see it) is that I wouldn't have known how to cope with seeing Cal flattened by my fists, and was obliged to perceive that there must now be considered a new dimension to our relationship. I didn't want either to defeat her or to humiliate her. I just wanted to salvage what I could of the wonderful relationship that once we had. So victory in battle over her wasn't in my best interests. I had been declining to wrestle, and I certainly wasn't going to start punching her. But when she enveloped me in a loosely clinging envelope of flesh, I permitted her superior weight to lower me to the ground. So she emerged from the contest confidently reasserting that I wasn't nearly as strong as my young cousin Nick, who was even younger than Chris in effect.

Another manner in which Cal asserted her psychological nuance of superiority over the rest of us was in her claim to preternatural sensitivity. My father's mother had exercised control over her family in this fashion, in a manner that Henry had always both believed and admired. So this thought may not have been too far from Cal's mind when she started to exercise such control over ourselves.

It required, of course, that she should have acquired some personal experience of viewing the ghosts who were resident at Longleat, and such stories did gradually accumulate. She told us how she had seen – Well, I won't go into all that, since my purpose is not to persuade my reader that there are indeed any ghosts at Longleat. But Cal had managed to see unsubstantiated spectral forms at Longleat, such as Henry was prepared to regard as evidence that she had inherited Violet's extrasensory powers. I, on the other hand, just felt left out, in that I never managed to see any of these things. And in each telling of her tales I noted how the detail in her stories became increasingly firm and irrefutable. In this manner, the ghosts of Longleat did have substance in our lives.

Then there was the game of planchette, at which Cal also excelled. I say that she excelled because the spirit that we summoned always managed to speak with the voice that she might desire – although usually she was just making fun of us, using lips other than her own. I can remember one instance of real terror when the upturned wine-glass, ringed as it was by letters, and with a finger from each of us extended to make supposedly superficial contact with its base, began to answer the question (proposed to the spirit by Cal) as to how we should lay it to rest, with the letters 'C U T (pause) O F F (pause) C H R I S ... '

Poor Chris was now cringing under the table, and even I didn't wish to see the message completed. But Cal insisted that we continue, after all the heart palpitations had subsided, until the message was reduced to an anticlimax in that the instruction became nothing worse than cutting off the top of a Christmas tree in Longleat woods.

I did notice, however, that the spirits Cal summoned to play with us at planchette had a knack of misspelling words in precisely the same manner as she did herself.

# Chapter 21

## Parents:
## Working towards reconciliation

Once Henry had surmounted his initial shock in discovering just how unfaithful Daphne had been to him during his absence in the Middle East, they had worked out a *modus vivendi*, putting in quite an effort to make the marriage work. Even so, I remained oblivious of just how close they had come to divorcing over those initial months. I remember one conversation in particular, with my school friend **[X]** (Romeo) when he came to stay with us in the holidays, about the impossibility that either set of parents would ever see fit to divorce. I simply didn't imagine that they might contemplate such an issue. I had the feeling that our home environment was so definitely secure.

Nor did I then see fit to connect Henry's fierce reassertion of dominance within the household as related to the idea that he was feeling cuckolded in his absence. I dare say that they were both now having sexual relationships on the side, but as far as the domestic scene was concerned, Henry was back there in the command seat, in a manner which Daphne accepted without demur.

The idea of being posted as an instructor at Bovington for the remainder of the war had never appealed to my father greatly. The piece of shrapnel that had been lodged briefly in his chest during the battle of El Alamein could not account for the fact that he had not been permitted to rejoin his regiment. In effect, he had been passed over, and the command of the Royal Wiltshire Yeomanry had been now entrusted to someone junior to himself. He felt both dissatisfied and offended at this outcome, and desired to play a more active part in the war.

Daphne in the meantime had offered her services to the American hospital, which was then being constructed in the park at Longleat. The American forces had been flooding into Britain in preparation for the opening of a second front – in Normandy, as it eventually transpired. And Longleat was the site chosen for one of their principal hospitals for convalescent servicemen. Daphne was appointed the official librarian, and she would sometimes take us along with her, to push her book trolley and to accompany her to lunch in the mess. She claimed that I put her to shame on one occasion by spitting out all the pieces of gristle from my beefburger and leaving them in a ring around the circumference of my plate.

The American connection made quite a big difference to all of our lives. American attitudes were so different from our own – more effusive and unreserved – and the men exuded a brash opulence such as we had been raised to conceal from public view, or even from our own recognition. Moreover, they were lavish with their presents, whether this amounted to toys or to chewing gum. Henry repaid their hospitality by inviting them to join his shooting parties, and there was the occasional dinner party at Sturford for them too.

Hospitality remained as lavish as ever, incidentally. Daphne's lovers might have emptied Henry's cellar during the period he had been away in Africa, but there was replenishment available – in terms of all the port that had been laid down at my birth and originally intended for my own consumption after marriage. (Such had been the family tradition over successive generations.) This treasure trove was promptly sequestered to my father's use, to compensate him for his own depleted cellar.

It was through his liberality as a host at Sturford that Henry now became friendly with General Pete Corlett, who was among those Americans in Britain who had been designated to lead the 9th army when they finally went into battle on the other side of the Channel. The idea of having a real live English aristocrat on his staff may have been something which appealed to General Corlett. Anyway, Henry gleefully accepted the post of liaison officer when it was offered to him. Not that it was ever really specified with whom it was that he was intended to liaise – a question that was put to him without satisfactory answer on the occasion when General Montgomery came to visit Pete Corlett. The idea was more that Henry might prove useful in a whole number of ways, if only to enhance the social status of the American general's headquarters.

The months while we were all waiting for the invasion of Normandy coincide with the peak of my hero-worship for Daddy – for all of us brothers, I dare say.

Caroline's excellent relationship with Henry was of a different kind. She was treated more in avuncular fashion, and as more of an adult, of course. But it was notable that even little Val was now striving his utmost to discover what he had been missing in this idea of a paternal relationship. All three of us boys would accompany my father, whenever it was permitted, on his trips out to inspect what was going on around the estate. Henry liked to be seen checking up on things in a highly personal style of management. He had always criticised his own father, incidentally, for his impersonal manner of running the estate through the services of an agent.

Val appeared in some ways troubled by the whole business of fitting a father into his life. It must have been evident to him that Nanny wasn't quite the impregnable redoubt that he might once have hoped, but then there was nobody else who could be relied upon to champion his cause like her. He was the runt of the litter, and neither Mummy nor Daddy were especially interested in supervising his situation in life. There were even facetious jokes by Henry about his real name once having been chosen as 'Gillian' – because he was 'Mr Gill's son'. Val was to tell me later how he could never tell if this information was intended to be taken as true or false.

In hindsight, I have more to add.

Despite the fact that such words were always uttered as a joke, I think it may have reflected an anxiety current in Henry's mind. I was to question him, many years later, about rumours I'd heard circulating in London about Val's not actually being his son. He replied in effect that he did have his doubts upon this matter, and that they were based upon 'something your mother once said to me in a fit of anger ... We were quarrelling at the time.'

It is not much for me to go by, but I am inferring that what he meant was that around the time of his return from Africa, during the explosive conversations which followed his discovery of the full extent of Daphne's infidelities, he may have enquired about the paternity of all his children. I know not how Daphne replied, but it would have been in character if she had taunted him a bit – if only to get back at him for the injustice of his accusation. It could well be that she told him that she couldn't know for sure if Val was his son. But whether this uncertainty was genuine or not, I have no means of telling, nor whether Henry did, at this time, have any serious doubt on the subject. Where I am certain is that he never thought for a single instant that Valentine had been fathered by Mr Gill.

The arena of humour was never a safe one between Henry and myself, any more than it was with Val. With Chris, it could be that my father encountered a safer streak of appreciation. I might be the wrong person to analyse this correctly, but I'd say that his feeling of humour needed to be triggered by an empathy of stepping inside Henry's shoes and reading an incongruity from that position. My own concern about what factually should be regarded as true or false might possibly have been a hindrance in my appreciation of his wit. But of course in this instance it was Val who was suffering rather than me.

I am going to stress the word 'facetious' (or inappropriate) in any reference to Henry's humour. It did require that you accepted him for what he was, and then became sensitive to all the ripples of mirthful incongruity which surrounded him. But if you fell out of line with that way of thinking, then you might brush up against some rougher aspects, finding yourself an object to be teased, or even bullied, according to whether the feeling of good humour lasted within himself.

Inasmuch that Henry was the model to whose image I wanted most of all to conform, I was always striving to feel my way to a full understanding of what I ought to be doing, or saying, to merit his sparkle of merriment. But usually when I was trying to be funny I somehow got it wrong, and I was aware how nobody really laughed. I was a slow starter in developing anything akin to my own brand of humour.

When the invasion of Normandy finally took place, we were back at school for the summer term. There were feelings of enormous excitement everywhere, for this was the battle we'd all been waiting for. It also furnished the boys at Ludgrove with the nearest we'll ever get to having front seats in witnessing an aerial cavalry charge. It may have been D-day plus the odd day or so when we trooped out on Mr Barber's front lawn one evening to gaze up at a sky filled with gliders on tow towards the coast – and France. There was a real feeling that they were all charging into battle, and the sky was simply full of them.

I can still feel a lump of emotion swelling in my throat at my recollection of this scene. Henceforward we were going to have the Huns on the run.

But of course it did mean that Daddy went off to the battle front once again, and I was enormously proud of him – fantasising upon the heroic exploits that he might be performing. And it wasn't very long before we learnt that he had been awarded the bronze star, which I persuaded myself was somewhere close to the Military Cross in equivalent merit. I wrote to him eagerly urging him to divulge how many Germans he had killed. His modesty on this subject had always been confusing. He had once been at pains to explain to me that when you give the order for a shell to be fired from a tank, you're not very certain just how many people it may (or may not) have killed – let alone the fact that it is not actually your own finger on the trigger. But I eventually elicited from him that he might, perhaps, have killed three Germans – and I was prepared to settle for that, informing all those of my friends who had enquired.

Daphne continued with her librarian activities at the American hospital, while keeping the home fires burning at Sturford. In some ways she had always been a more constant presence in the family, yet I was aware at the same time how there was something peculiarly inconstant in her nature. She lacked that quality of being like the metaphorical rock upon which anyone could safely build. But I still felt enormously warm towards her, and knew that she esteemed me well. With Henry it was always a huge challenge to earn his esteem, but with Daphne I knew that I had it – even when it was unearned.

One of the most delightful aspects of Daphne's charm was her aura of slightly batty femininity. There was little sense of strict logic beneath her whimsical enthusiasms, but they all gave colour to her entertaining personality. An anecdote might illustrate the point.

Daphne enjoyed the occasional small flutter on the horses, but she was also superstitious, and once she had struck upon some successful way of courting Lady Luck, she pursued that method relentlessly – well, for a week or so, in any case. For a while she attributed all her recent winnings upon the divine intervention of Bacchus, who surveyed the drawing-room window from his white marble pedestal at the far end of the front lawn. So before placing any further bets, Mummy would rush over to perform a short ritual of obeisance, which involved her pouring a small libation of wine into his bird-stained lips and then over his lichened feet. It was a habit she discontinued, however, the day she looked up from her reverences to perceive that the new head gardener, who had been trimming the yew hedge with a pair of clippers from the other side, stood there peering over the top of it, distinctly curious at her antics. Daphne hesitated for a moment, and then waved the emptied wine glass vaguely in the air. 'It's a sort of game,' she explained, before retiring sheepishly towards the drawing-room.

My attitude towards Daphne had by now become stricken with an uncertainty concerning how I ought to be judging her – and I am here talking about sitting in moral judgement. My intuitive antennae had picked up the message that there were those who regarded her as a bit of a scarlet woman. But my own feelings of loyalty towards her were still paramount. Perhaps I sensed that her position wasn't exactly a safe one. Perhaps I was asking myself whether, in the event of her being offered up as an expendable sacrifice, my own fate might not turn out to be bound up inextricably with hers.

The ambivalence in my attitude shows up in a poem that I sent her at this time. I may have thought that I was displaying my potential as a ballad writer, but it strikes me now that I was trying to communicate something deeper than that.

> One day a dame slipped out of bed
> and, over some small strife,
> she severed through her husband's head
> by slashing with a knife.
>
> And then at once she told her son
> to mind he didn't say
> about her deed to anyone
> until she'd passed away.
>
> She said that if it got afloat,
> she'd take the knife again,
> and plunge it deep into his throat,
> and split it up in twain.
>
> Unknown to her, a man had passed
> when she had done her crime.
> With eyes aflame, he'd watched aghast,
> and stayed there quite a time.
>
> Then off he'd run to find some men
> to catch this vile female;
> to find her first, arrest her, then

to cart her off to jail.

They went and found her in her bed,
and forced her and her son
to follow to the place they led
by showing her a gun.

They locked the prisoners up in jail
and outside left as guard
a tough and brawny, thick-set male
with muscles big and hard.

But there inside that beastly cell,
the mother sat with glee
while vowing that she'd eat, as well,
her little son for tea.

So thereupon, with every ounce
of strength she ever had,
the wicked mother made a pounce
upon the luckless lad.

She then proceeded, with great greed,
to take his eyes and tongue,
and ate them. So for these few deeds,
the wicked wretch was hung.

At this distance in time, let me now pose as a psychiatrist concerned to analyse the anxieties that the young poet may have been striving to express. The mother's crime is that she 'severs through' her husband's head, which is a clear case of symbolic castration, or cuckolding. The son's crime is that he bore witness to this cuckolding, but had been sworn to silence on the issue. Nonetheless, he gets taken to the house of punishment alongside her. Once there, however, he finds that his eyes which had born witness to the mother's crime, and his tongue which might always speak out about it, were now objects which she might wish to destroy in him. He perceives this as the potential destruction of his identity. But it is she who remains, ultimately, the real guilty party and she is obliged to pay the full penalty for her misdeeds.

Another way of looking at it is to say that the verses display a remarkable deterioration in my conception of motherhood since the days when I had penned those stanzas which began:

> Oh, the little foal has play,
> while his mother works all day ...

But I was growing up, of course.

While uncertainty may have been gathering in my attitude towards Daphne, my attitude towards Henry was to absorb as much of his identity as I possibly could. And I was enormously perturbed, at the time of the Runstedt breakthrough in the Ardennes, that he might be killed. It was a stroke of good fortune that he had been back at home with us on a short spell of leave when the offensive had initially been launched, and when most of the casualties had been inflicted. But he had returned immediately to the front (leaving me sobbing at night in my bed, I might add). And the situation emerged after arriving back at General Pete Corlett's headquarters when, with the Germans still advancing, he was sent to demobilise American trucks, only to find that the enemy were already on the premises. His cool behaviour in pretending not to have observed that they were observing him, while continuing to supervise the demobilisation of the trucks, won him the Silver Star (to add to his Bronze Star), and I now truly felt that I was the genetic offspring of a war hero.

*GI News* article from *Hank the Yank*, by Cecil Carnes:

### Major the Viscount Weymouth, next Marquess of Bath, leads his brace of pet ducks along the western front on a leash, and thereby qualifies as the GIs' pet British officer

LT.-COL. GEORGE FORSYTHE, of Gregson Springs, Montana, quickly picked a squad of soldiers from the drivers, cooks, clerks and signalmen about him. He led them into the tall ferns a few hundred yards from the corps command post, then not far from the German border. Then captured five German officers and 148 men who had blundered in there during the night. There followed a long, triumphant procession through the camp with an MP rear-guard smoking a big cigar and bowing right and left to his pals. And trailing them all came a tall, thin British major, walking with two ducks on a leash of string.

Busy officers and men looked up, smiled, and added a friendly wave for the man with the ducks. To a stranger it would have been a scene worthy of a double-take in the Hollywood manner. After all, this was within the sound of battle. And the little Muscovy ducks had humps on their noses just where their master had one on his. Ducks and master moved with a waddling saunter which should have told the world, 'Watch out for three uninhibited characters.'

But to those who knew the folkways of the corps, this was almost SOP – standard operational procedure. They could have told you, with pride, how the tall British major and his duck pets had turned up in the strangest places; how they had given tone to the 19th Corps; how their adventures provided a living, day-to-day, comic newsreel.

They had written many a letter home about this single-ring circus at the war. Many a story had appeared in the corps' mimeographed newspaper. Thus the group of energetic AWVS workers in New York City, who had 'adopted' the 19th Corps, took official notice of the ducks.

On the very day of that procession through the camp, Mrs A. J. Stone went to a sporting-goods store and picked up a special present she'd ordered some weeks before. It was a couple of tiny duck collars attached to one split-leather leash, the only one of its kind ever made. Mrs Stone addressed the gift to Major the Viscount Weymouth, known as Henry, or 'Hank the Yank'. She and her associates have equipped Henry, who will be the next Marquess of Bath, with the gear he needed to put his ducks in the victory parade down Unter den Linden.

His American friends have no doubt that Henry will parade if the notion strikes him, and if the ducks, Don Juan and Yvonne, are in health. For Henry is absolutely at ease with the world at all times. In any compendium of unforgettable characters, he would rate an honoured spot near the top of the list. Americans are delighted with him not only because he is the screwball they'd always imagined a titled

Englishman ought to be – even though he doesn't wear a monocle – but because he also is the kind of two-fisted guy you'd like to have beside you in an alley brawl on a dark night. He would be famous for his bravery if it weren't for the fact that he has already been acclaimed the most beloved eccentric who ever tried to drink his binoculars while looking through his canteen.

Henry, forty years of age and convalescing from wounds received in action in Syria, had met the officers of the 19th Corps back in England. He and his father, the eighty-two-year-old Marquess of Bath, had entertained them at his comfortable place, Sturford Mead, and his father's famous estate, Longleat, near Warminster, Wiltshire. The Americans had been intrigued by Henry's enthusiastic misuse of American slang and his nostalgic recollections of a trip to Texas in 1924. He had roamed the plains around Amarillo, was soundly hazed by cowhands and loved it. Ever since, he confesses, there has been a touch of Texas in his blood.

'Like the blokes who read the football tallies in your country,' Henry explains, 'and become alumni of Notre Dame through a sort of sympathetic reaction, my friends are teasing me now for my affinity toward Americans. They call me "Hank the Yank". Tie that for a basin of bah-nah-nahs!'

The Americans borrowed 'Hank the Yank' as a name for Henry. They liked the fact that Henry had a flattened beak from boxing. They learned Henry shoots (hunts) and hunts (rides). And while Henry was strictly old-school-tie – Harrow – his Yankee friends learned he had stood for Parliament in 1931, and been elected by the largest majority ever given a candidate from his constituency. One term had been enough for Henry, because he could see war coming any time after 1935. Holding a commission in the territorial army, he settled back to training, spending time with Lady Weymouth and their four charming children, three boys and a girl, in the Longleat library, which houses one of the finest private collections in England. There Henry showed his American friends original Chaucers and Caxtons, the first folio Shakespeares, and the letter written by Lord Derby to Queen Elizabeth advising Her Majesty that Mary, Queen of Scots, was well and truly dead.

While the Americans were near by, Henry took keen interest in their training for the invasion of Europe. As D-day drew near, some of the younger American officers decided to stage a polite kidnapping of Henry for the battle of France. Henry knew of the schemes, and they pleased him immensely. But kidnapping did not turn out to be necessary. Maj. Gen. Charles H. Corlett, the 'Cowboy Pete' who, as a character right out of America's great Southwest, delighted Henry, applied for a British liaison officer for the 19th Corps. He asked for, and got, Lord Weymouth, alias Hank the Yank.

Major the Viscount Weymouth showed up at camp wearing a pair of GI pants, British field boots and an American combat jacket bearing the crown of a British major and the insignia of the 19th Army Corps, a toma-hawk. Perched on his thinning brown hair was a Montgomery beret, very black, sporting the badge of the Royal Wiltshire Yeomanry, a regiment founded by that particular Marquess of Bath who was his great-grandfather.

Henry hit the beachhead from a PT boat in company with two generals, six colonels and another major. Figuring himself outranked, he immediately took over the mess. He was, as he happily put it, 'a natural' for this sort of hanky-panky, since he spoke French. He went through the countryside, scrounging and mooching. Butter, chickens and eggs quickly replaced K-rations. Henry was right on the beam when groping through the chicken roosts of France.

It was in one profitable barnyard that his heart was taken by a pair of Muscovy ducks. Recalling what lovely pets they made, he promptly bought them. Now, at this time, the beachhead wasn't a great real-estate development – we had a battle lien on a small section of France and had to throw our entire weight in to hold it. So shells were landing almost everywhere. Henry named his ducks 'Yvonne' and 'Don Juan,' unfolded his portable canvas bathtub – the one he called 'my family shield' – and set the ducks up in house-keeping. One of the ducks was larger than the other. This one, he reasoned, was a drake. It was only natural, therefore, that when he exercised them, the drake should go ahead, as Henry put it, 'feeling out the mines which might cook his goose, or rather, duck.' It may have been the war, but both Yvonne and Don Juan turned out to be highly excitable. Henry had to anchor them by strings attached to their legs. He was confident that after a few days of food and affection they would grow domesticated, matching the lovely pets he had made out of his well-mannered English Muscovys.

All this time Henry was going up to the front daily. He was on duty with the combat observer section of corps headquarters, and his idea of how to check enemy positions was to stroll over and look in on the German positions in person. After the sun went down, he would come back and enjoy his ducks. I remember the first time I saw him. Henry and I were listening to the artillery pounding not far away. 'I let the ducks take a walk by themselves at dusk,' Henry said. 'I thought it was the democratic thing to do.' One of the generals commanding a division strolled over and began explaining a tactical problem for the next day. It was rather an involved situation for a novice like myself, but Henry grasped it at once. After he had listened to the general for ten minutes or so, Henry said politely, 'I think I hear them now.' I could hear nothing but the plunging, exploding shells. Henry walked through the darkness along the hedgerows and recovered his ducks.

Next day, the corps headquarters moved. Profiting by his long experience in the field in Africa and the Middle East, Henry paid attention to the little niceties of living, and by careful attention to details he managed to minimize the inconvenience of war. He had the use of a captured German Opel touring car, loudly painted with the Allied star so it might easily be identified by Allied pilots. To Hank, Opel was short for opulence, and even though the car inevitably broke down – after ten miles, as certainly as if it had been guaranteed by a Broadway sharpy – he wouldn't trade it for any number of other assemblies he was offered.

So this corny joke of a car was run alongside the wall tent which Henry shared with Capt. Lloyd. L. McDaniel, of Decatur, Illinois. Into its comfortably upholstered rear

Henry put a cardboard miniature of a Pullman section. That was for Yvonne and Don Juan. Then Henry packed in his red dressing-gown and carpet-slippers, his two foot lockers, a supply of American D-ration vitamin-packed chocolate bars, on which he dotes and hopes to gain weight right in the middle of a war, his fleece-lined sleeping bag – the only one in the corps – a market basket (the one in which he packs his lunch when he goes out to the battlefield), a tripod, and a very, very white washbasin. Next he put in Henri, his nice, red-cheeked French valet, a kid who had volunteered for the job and who had found it no mean task to ride herd on two ducks of the uninhibited type and an equally uninhibited duck lover. Henri had been outfitted – quartermasters, please look the other way – with American GI clothing. So they took off, and after the customary number of breakdowns – the number of miles divided by ten equals the perverse ratio of the motor – they reached the meadow where the command post was to be established.

Here Hank dropped things and went about his business of 'liaising', after taking his ducks for a short leg-stretching stroll. And here a visiting inspector of camouflage dropped around. He stopped in his tracks and stared at his lordship's collapsible washstand, holding aloft the brightest, shiningest, whitest porcelain basin that ever graced a battle front. His red face turned to mauve – a menacing mauve. And then he called to a lieutenant – the very nearest one.

'Whose', he demanded, 'is that?'

'Why, sir, that – that is Henry's.'

'Oh. And doesn't Henry care what happens to the Nineteenth Corps? Doesn't he know a Luftwaffe pilot could spot that damned thing from twenty thousand feet? You tell Henry to smash that thing and bury the pieces!'

'Sir,' the lieutenant offered, 'that might lead to serious – I might say, international – consequences. Why – '

'Have you got trouble here with a bunch of goofs?' the major asked. 'Well, I know how it is when you run into bad luck in a corps. Like, for instance, when I was coming in here, my jeep passed a guy who was actually leading a couple of ducks on a string. Forget it! Cut some branches off the nearest tree and tie them to the main tent pole, so they over-hang this prominent bit of equipment. I know what it is to live among crazy people. I live in Los Angeles!'

And he was off on his rounds, leaving a young lieu-tenant joyful because Henry's style hadn't been cramped. That feeling about Henry was universally shared. Ordinarily, liaison officers are appointed for some linking mission, say between the British 2nd Army and the American 1st or between the British 30th Corps and the American 19th, or 7th, or whatever. But only for a specific task. Then they are recalled. Now, Henry was not to be trammelled by such restrictions. The corps commanders wanted him to liaise in all directions. But they knew he was probably the only liaison officer-at-large. There was, there-fore, some anxiety when Field Marshal – then General – Sir Bernard L. Montgomery visited the corps headquarters and met Major the Viscount Weymouth.

'What do you do?' inquired Montgomery showing just the correct interest.

'Major Weymouth is our liaison officer,' interposed General Corlett hurriedly.

'Who does he liaise between?' asked Monty casually.

Henry started to harrumph a bit, but General Corlett was equal to the situation, tactically. He remarked quickly that Henry liaised with whoever was on their flank, and in addition was assistant G-3 – Operations. Monty looked a bit bewildered by this explanation, but it obviously was a position he couldn't attack without his famous massed artillery. His conversational guns being spiked, the subject was re-rifled, successfully.

It was merely a coincidence, but the very next day Henry had a chance to show that it took more than charm and a penchant for making friends to keep him in business. He and Lt.-Col.Thomas L. Crystal, Jr, of Washington, DC were reconnoitring at the front for a promising-looking command-post site. The Germans sent a force through west of Tessy-sur-Vire and cut them off. To the very conservative Henry, it looked like a mere patrol. Actually, it was a full company of crack German infantry and a platoon of tanks.

Henry and his driver went to the right and Colonel Crystal and his driver went to the left. They were going to set up a small cross-fire, if practicable. When Henry discovered the true size of the enemy force and inspected their defensive positions covering the road, he went home – on tiptoe. Having walked through the German lines and failing to find Colonel Crystal back at corps headquarters, Henry returned and did some more gumshoe work up and down behind the Germans. No Crystal. So back to camp. Henry took Yvonne and Don Juan for a long walk, just to get his mind off the colonel's disappearance. And, of course, ran into the colonel riding back in someone else's jeep. He had stayed, surreptitiously, with the Germans, in order to finish sketches of their installations.

The next thing the Germans thought up for the 19th Corps was the Gethsemane of Gathemo. They launched a counter-offensive in great force north of Mortain. Henry got very much enthused by the manner in which the Americans contained this drive. He wound up every day as an integral part of the front lines. When word came to General Corlett about this, he called Henry before him. In the little trailer office where he maps his plans, General Corlett said, 'Henry, I hear you have been neglecting your ducks. From now on, you will go no farther than battalion command posts, so you can get back to your tent earlier. A dead duck of a liaison officer is no good to me.'

Just the same, Henry was given the American Bronze Star for bravery. King George has to approve all decorations received by British officers. While Henry's American medal was working its way through Buckingham Palace, the King suddenly came though with a Territorial Efficiency Medal. When news of this reached General Corlett's mess, where Henry and the other officers of the corps family eat their meals, Lord Weymouth hastily volunteered an explanation. 'It's just a routine decoration,' said Henry, 'awarded all who have not disgraced themselves in twenty years.' The staff officers pretended there was only one explanation: King George was just trying to wean Henry away from the 19th Corps.

'There is a dirty ring here, too, surrounding our Bath,' quipped Maj. Roy D. Craft, editor of the corps newspaper, 'suggesting duck with Free-French fries would be character-building. Let us nip this campaign in the very taste buds. Especially is such talk subversive, as Henry, heady with liberation here in France, is about to unleash Don Juan and Yvonne.'

The day Henry decided to free his ducks was one of the frequent headquarters moving-days. He loosed the strings from their legs. Yvonne immediately soared aloft, gracefully cleared a line of 100-foot trees and vanished forever. Don Juan sat around for a time, then went aloft in the slipstream of his girl-friend. Sadly, Henry loaded his Opel and drove off for the new CP site, thinking never to see either of the Muscovys again.

Don Juan, however, came back to the old CP at the usual time for chow – to find the place deserted. He was hissing his disgust when the corps chief of staff chanced to come back for something. The general tossed Don into a gunny sack, piled maps and brief cases on top of him and drove to the new post. Here Don Juan waddled indignantly out of the sack, and without so much as a look at his fond master, took off out of Henry's life.

But in less than four hours, Henry was given their successors, two tiny ducklings. Again, assuming the larger to be a drake and the smaller a duck, he named them Don Juan and Yvonne, in memory of those earlier friendships. And Henry worked on their emotions from the very start. It was something to watch when he took them out for a stroll, with cannon pounding a short distance ahead, the ducklings walking in single file, the larger leading the way. They went all through France and Belgium like that, making a big hit with the civilian population. Some of the children even offered the ducks tastes of the bonbons they had been given by the American soldiers. Henry and his web-footed friends were inseparable. He would unleash them and they would walk long distances, but always come back. Henry claimed that his 'poultry patrol' had often penetrated tough Nazi defenses.

One day up near the German border, the command post was established on the grounds of an ancient château. Through the moat flowed a swift-moving stream of ice-cold mountain water. On the banks waited a husky, energetic, chocolate-colored puppy named St Lô, after the battle-scarred town where he was found immediately after the Americans broke through.

St Lô had been getting all of everyone's attention until this last set of cute ducklings came along. As for Yvonne and Don Juan, they hissed like a busted steam pipe as they strutted past St Lô. He retaliated by catching the Muscovys in an unguarded moment and driving them into the brook.

He kept them there, paddling desperately against the rapid, icy current. Barking furiously, he raced back and forth, heading them off whenever they tried a landing. They were at the point of exhaustion when an enlisted man rowed out and brought them ashore. But when he put them on the ground, they couldn't stand up. They fell down and lay helplessly paralyzed for days. St Lô was disgraced. But Major Craft, his owner, said the pup felt bad about the whole thing, and hinted at extenuating circumstances – combat fatigue and war nerves, coupled with exhaustion in trying to catch up with the retreating Germans. In the corps newspaper, *Le Tomahawk*, he expressed his hope that the incident wouldn't be allowed to affect Anglo-American relations.

'At least not ours and Henry's,' he wrote. 'When this war is over, we want to be on the best of terms with him, so we can visit his place and sit on a stick and shoot partridges while the hired hands drive them by.'

Finally, tender treatment brought the Muscovys back to health. One night not long ago, at the command post near the front, the staff officers were having dinner.

'Isn't that the whistle of German planes?' someone asked.

'Nope,' said Col. Carl Jones. 'You can tell them miles away.'

Whereupon there were the explosions of several aerial bombs just outside and the racket of diving Stukas.

'Yvonne!' gasped Henry. 'Don Juan! They're out!'

He ran through the blackness and the explosions, looking for his Muscovys. It was a much more dangerous thing
to do than removing a wounded man from the front lines in
daylight. Bombs burst all around. But in a short time,
Henry reappeared, smiling and ruffling the Muscovys' neck
feathers soothingly.

In the light of a faltering flashlamp, the brass hats
looked at one another and grinned as they heard the GI
cook say, 'Henry is a very fine Joe.'

There was a less healthy side to our relationship, however, in that Henry
was converted to fascism – by a colonel on General Corlett's staff. During
his spells of leave, he was concerned to make all his guests understand how
this was the new inspiration in his life, and I was listening with devout
attention to all that he uttered. It is important that I should analyse this
position in detail.

The manner in which Henry would present his case was roughly
as follows.

There was this colonel on the general's staff, and when he
was there in the mess, he would have the whole lot of us
arguing our heads off. But he knew what he was saying and
he would stick to his guns ... He kept telling us that we were
in the process of wiping out the finest nation in Europe.
'Look at their farms,' he would say. 'Do you ever see any
muck, or dirt? They are the best-kept farms that you'll ever
see. And we're in the process of trying to wipe these people
from the face of this earth. But of course, we've got to –
because we're at war with them. It's their neck, or ours.'

It was this colonel who advised me to take a closer look
at what Hitler had actually said. He told me to get hold of
an English translation of Mein Kampf, which I've done.
And I've got to admit that there's a lot of truth in what he
tells us ... I mean it's a fact of life that the wolf pack follows
its leader. The pack's success or failure depends upon the
wolf that's up there in front. If he's strong and cunning, they
go places, but if he's grown old and weak, then they all perish. We've all got to find someone intelligent and strong to
place up there in leadership. And once we've done this, we've

got to do what he says. We've got to follow him through thick and thin, in a spirit of undivided loyalty – until he grows old and weak, that is to say. Then we have to take the ruthless decision to put someone else up there in his place, switching our loyalties to him instead.

Little by little, Henry became far fiercer in his endorsement of fascism, especially after the general election when Atlee replaced Churchill as Prime Minister, during the final stages of the war. His line then would run as follows.

There's democracy for you! Churchill did all the spadework to bring us victory. But when he goes to the people and asks them to show their gratitude by voting him another term of office, they throw him out. Someone's out there promising them quick riches, and they get sucked in. They believe all that rubbish. That's the people for you! If you're going to allow them to take crucial decisions, you'll land up in every manner of mess.

Then someone might probe whether Henry's foremost admiration was for Churchill, or for Hitler. To that, his line of reply was:

Well, it's got to be Hitler. I mean he took on the entire world, and he damn nearly won. You've got to be a genius to come so close to victory in that kind of situation. Churchill did all right, but he had all the advantages stacked on his side. And when you come down to it, his one claim to fame is that he finally managed to defeat Hitler. There's little else that he'll go down in history for. He didn't get a chance for that – not under a system when he's always got to go cap in hand to the people and ask them for another term in office. Under democracy, he gets slung out.

The subject of fascist outrages would often arise, and an apology demanded for acts of brutal suppression in countries occupied by the Axis powers, or for the programme for racial purification in the extermination of Jews. With regard to the former, Henry would argue that ruthlessness was necessary (and admirable) at times when you were fighting with your back against the wall.

> You can't blame the Germans for acting like that, when they
> had the whole world lined up against them. The alternative
> was to chuck in the sponge just as soon as the going got
> tough. But that would have been out of character for Hitler,
> and we must admire him for it.

On the question of ethno-religious purification, it is best that I say as little
as possible. Henry would deny that the deaths were as numerous as were
rumoured. Then he would appeal for a consensus of opinion that the world
hadn't really lost anything from the death of a few Jews. Some basic streak
of anti-Semitism was emerging from his subconscious, prompting him to
credit his political hero with the concoction of a spurious rationale for their
elimination from the human scene.

But it was in the justification of right-wing political thinking versus left
that Henry's conversion to fascism gave rise to his most eloquent tirades.
What to do with the striking dockers, or miners, for example?

> Just put their leaders up against the wall, and tell them to go
> back to work – or else ... And if they're still refusing to lis-
> ten, then you bloody well shoot them. And I can promise
> you that there won't be anyone talking about strike action
> after that!

Daphne did nothing to encourage him within his fascist views, and she
joined in the general chorus of protest against the inhumanity of so many
of his utterances. But she did little to expound a contrary thesis for my
understanding. To my ears it always sounded as if Dad was setting out to
be true to himself, presenting unpopular ideas against all opposition. I
admired his boldness, and it was the only coherent case that was ever
argued in my presence. So I gradually got the feel of his position, and
began to absorb it as my own.

But this was really a period of rapprochement between Henry and
Daphne. While he preened himself, and pirouetted in his new-found elo-
quence, she welcomed in effect that she was back under the domination of
a virile masculine influence – and they were possibly even sexually faithful
to one another, for the time being. Any thought that the ideas Henry was
feeding me might be unhealthy for my burgeoning personality was never

even considered. In all probability, Daphne felt that I was now quite old enough to take care of myself.

Mention should be made of two deaths on my mother's side of the family. The first was Granny McCalmont, my mother's mother's mother (and my own great-grandmother, of course). She finally died after a short illness, at the age of well over ninety. I had always been her favourite grandchild, ever since the days when she would come and sit at my bedside while I was recovering from that mastoid operation in the London hospital. I was the only one in our family to whom she bequeathed anything in her will. This took the form of a painting attributed to Zoffany, which experts ultimately pronounced to be an oleograph, not an oil painting, and in all probability by one of his pupils rather than by the master himself. But the intention was there, and I still feel grateful (and affectionate) towards her.

The second death was that of Grandpa George Vivian, my mother's father. There was an ageing gun-dog which survived him by a few days – so old that the decision had been taken that it should be put down. So George took him out on what was intended as a last walk in the woods, so that he could be shot while enjoying life to the full, at some distance from the house. A shot was indeed heard, and my step-Granny, Nancy, awaited her husband's sorrowful return. But it was the dog who returned, wagging his tail and as full of life as ever. A search party later discovered George lying with gun in hand, and deceased. The emotional crisis in pulling that trigger had brought on a cardiac arrest, fouling up his aim into the bargain.

# Chapter 22

## Activities:
## A modest first flowering

It was a somewhat secluded world for all of us children at Sturford, by which I mean that we had few friends living in the immediate vicinity. I think I had fewer than the others. Chris in particular had more local chums, partly because our Wilson cousins now came to live at the Pheasantry, which was a house in the park. (My Aunt Mary was by then divorced from John, Lord Numburnholm, and had remarried to Sir Ulrick Alexander.) Charlie Wilson was only slightly younger than Chris, and was now at Ludgrove after first attending the Lord Weymouth School. Nick Vivian had by then also joined them at Ludgrove, and sometimes came to stay at Sturford. There was also Dickie Rawlings, the son of the local publican. So there was quite a small gang of them, in whose ranks I was never fully integrated.

On the occasions we did band together, I dare say it's true that I was a bad influence over them. It worries me to think how we used to ambush cars from the security of the undergrowth up on top of a steep bank overlooking the main road which bordered the water garden at Sturford, firing stones from catapults – usually directed at the rear window of a car which had passed us by. Mercifully, there were no accidents. But there was one occasion when an irate driver slammed on his brakes, and then climbed the bank to pursue us. We scattered to different hiding-places within the shrubberies, and it was only Chris who got caught, to receive the full verbal blast of his wrath. It did have the salubrious effect, however, of dissuading us from such activities in future.

My interests were usually of a more gentle variety.

I was still fascinated by wild life, whether in the form of insects, fishes, reptiles, birds or mammals. There was a group of us at Ludgrove (consisting mainly of Iain Grahame-Wigan, Anthony Casdagli, Mark Dent-Brocklehurst and myself) who were concerned to study nesting birds, and we kept a pet jackdaw – until it got eaten by the gardener's cat. Snakes and lizards also featured within our secret menagerie. Slow-worms and grass snakes featured for the most part, but there were some exciting sightings of smooth snakes within the rough terrain of what went by the name of 'the wilderness'. But I hardly think the RSPCA would have approved the conditions under which the creatures we actually captured were caged.

I also acquired a small reputation within the school for what might be described as my gamekeeper skills – the art of trapping moles, in particular. When Ali's front lawn was stricken with molehills, it was my services which were called upon to restore the turf to its former beauty. And I discovered in the process that there was a rare variant of mole dwelling in that district, with distinctive skewbald patches of orange upon their black pelts.

My collection of butterflies and moths was a good one for someone of my age, and I sometimes wrote home about my activities in that field – somewhat ambiguously, as the letters now read. Take this one, for example.

> I have caught an old lady this week. I had a lot of trouble killing her, for she escaped several times before I was able to pinch her thorax. To my horror I saw, while I was setting her, that she was alive and wriggling, but afterwards I found that it was only nerves.

For the benefit of the uninformed, an Old Lady is the name of a moth – something Daphne guessed, of course, after the initial moment of shock.

Scouting featured prominently upon the list of approved activities at Ludgrove. It furnished a welcome break from the routine of both work and sport, and was vastly less competitive than so many of our other activities. Not entirely, of course, and I was eventually appointed to be one of the Patrol Leaders, but it was the whole idea of getting back to nature which really appealed to me – not that I achieved much fulfilment in that direction.

Theatrical productions were rare at Ludgrove, and were usually operettas of the Gilbert and Sullivan genre, the cast limited to those who took singing lessons. I was indeed one of these, so I was allotted a leading part during my final year. My voice may have been good, but having to act as someone other than myself never came naturally to me. I can recollect but little of the storyline at this distance in time. I know that I was the captain's mate on board some ship that was later wrecked on a Pacific island, and that (prior to this) I was bullied into plugging the hole that had appeared below the Plimsoll-line with my rear end. I remember feeling disappointed that my Thespian prowess was not singled out for praise within the end of term reports.

I might not excel as an actor, but I still enjoyed theatrical stunts like going to fancy-dress parties, and there was one in Bath which I remember with pleasure. I had the idea of going as a one-legged pirate, with both of my legs stuffed down one side of my pyjamas and then into a large stocking, with a stout walking stick protruding from the other. I growled and grimaced my way into the final selection, and was in fact awarded one of the prizes, which I valued all the more in that Chris (as another pirate) received no such recognition.

Where I was managing to emerge with some small degree of excellence was in my literary ability. Encouraged by Mr Borgnis (or 'Borny-bug') who was the principal teacher of English at Ludgrove, I knew that my essays were expected to match, or to better, those written by the rest of the form. I had a vivid imagination, and was prepared to experiment with questions of style. I also regarded myself as a bit of a poet, often rounding off my letters back home with verses which, for the most part, were intended to be read humorously.

There was in fact an element of humour which was now emerging, for the first time, in my approach to life – although I might hesitate to commend its quality in retrospect. For it was really a question of discovering for myself the popularity, or source of amusement, which is credited to those who learn the art of undermining the heavy seriousness of education, to ribald effect. (An apology to my teachers is belatedly on offer!)

As I see it. the real culprit was Toad Morrison. (He was probably the most erudite of our Classics masters, but he did bear a remarkable resemblance to a toad, both facially and sartorially, in that he was slovenly, unkempt and perpetually blinking his eyes.) When I first moved up into his Classics division, I exercised the skills of my enquiring mind by asking a great number of questions. To the best of my retrospective belief they were posed originally in a spirit of sincerity, that I might more quickly reach an understanding of what was being taught. But Toad regarded these interruptions as a digression which distracted the attention of others. So he endeavoured to discourage me by poking fun at my insatiable curiosity.

'Twitter, twitter, twitter!' he would exclaim. 'Let us all stop to listen to the greater spotted clodhopper!' And there would be peals of laughter from all and sundry.

If his intention had been to discourage my antics, in effect it proved contrary. I suddenly discovered that I had manipulative control over their levels of mirth, and this was an entirely new experience for me. An element of clowning buffoonery now entered upon the motivation behind my questions, and I discovered that I was rather good at it, my performance poker-faced, if mischievous. At the encouragement of Toad, they would all scream 'Twitter! Twitter!' at me. But it was a rebuke that was delivered with affection, because they regarded it as some manner of enlivenment within the tedium of education. And this is a tale which needed to be told, if for no better reason that I acquired for myself at this juncture (and in place of 'Juliet') the nickname of 'Twitter' Thynne, which was inherited by both Christopher and Valentine in their turn.

In some ways however, the reputation of joker was an ill one to acquire. The quest for mirth in others began to pervade my attitude towards school activities in general, to an extent that I began to irritate people. I know that Borny-bug dropped me from the Ludgrove 3rd XI in soccer after he'd observed me clowning upon the field on receiving a hack upon my shins from an opponent appropriately named Legge. But the truth of the matter is that I never really was much good at playing football, so I cannot be confident that the reason stated was why he dropped me.

I was slightly better at cricket, however, and I enjoyed it more as well – if only for the reason that it was played in weather that I preferred. And during my final summer at Ludgrove I was appointed captain of the 2nd XI – proficient more as a bowler than as a batsman, but quite a good all-rounder within a team which could match the 1st XIs from various of the local preparatory schools.

The only sporting arenas in which I excelled were the gymnasium and the boxing ring. Perhaps as a result of his recently acquired admiration for 'true Aryan' values, Henry's concern had moved in the direction of physical fitness. He performed press-ups each morning when he was at home, and it occurred to me that in order to acquire his esteem I ought to match (or better) his performance. It didn't take me long to do just this. But after I surpassed his own best performance with I think twenty press-ups, his own interest in the fitness spree appeared to diminish. So it turned out to be a hollow achievement.

Nonetheless, I was an agile gymnast and a stylish pugilist. I had already upset the established form by defeating Ronnie Ferguson in an exhibition bout when the local army unit sent officers to instruct us on the techniques of judging and refereeing a contest. But it was never established whether I would in fact have dethroned Mark Jeffreys, who was the heavyweight school champion, during my final year because I went down with measles and chickenpox, in quick succession, shortly after emerging victorious from the semi-finals. But there were many who thought that I would have done so, if the match had ever been held.

In point of fact, I felt badly about failing to insist that the match be held during the final week of that Easter term, after I had emerged from the sick-room. With my reputation for guts, it might well have been expected of me – despite the comparative weakness of convalescence. I somehow supposed that the honours would be shared, in that the contest had never been resolved. It shamed me greatly when the moment of prize-giving arrived to find that I had lost out on the championship by default.

This question of guts should be examined more closely, for there has always been a streak of cowardice underlying – and perhaps inspiring – my determination to dare what I might otherwise seek to avoid. The issue revolves around my self-confidence, or my lack of it. Having been set up, relatively, upon a pinnacle from the moment of birth, I had in some ways been brought up to believe in myself wherever some spark of talent might be revealed. But in contrast to this tendency, my father had always been fiercely repressive, pouncing upon items of behaviour which did not conform to his own sense of order. This was inhibitive to the psychology of daring, and I was always having to surmount my caution in areas of uncertainty. And here was an instance where I felt in retrospect that I had let myself down, by not insisting that the boxing match be held.

The point is that I failed. I attended the scouts' camp at Barewood, and mounted the high diving board, along with one P. G. Holcroft. We both peered with some trepidation over the edge, but it was 'PG' who suddenly took the plunge – closely followed by myself, of course. But this amounted to a failure in matching up to Cabbage's prediction of aristocratic leadership, and I knew in my heart that I had let him down.

During my final year at Ludgrove, my scholarly interest was slipping. I think it is relevant for me to mention that the academic reputation of Ludgrove as a preparatory school recommended to parents who wished to send their sons to Eton, had also slipped badly since the period preceding the war, largely because its team of masters had been broken up for military service. The educational standard had plummeted, as shown up in the unprecedented percentage of low performance in the Common Entrance Examinations over recent years. It is a fact that the Eton authorities withdrew their special recommendation of Ludgrove as a preparatory school at around this time.

For whatever reason, however, my own concern about scholastic prowess lapsed over my final year – perhaps not least because I was now enjoying myself quite considerably at school, and was more concerned in savouring my mounting popularity and prestige as a personality. Also my prolonged confinement to the sick-room with measles and chickenpox over my penultimate term at Ludgrove did little to sharpen my intellect at the moment when such grading was to be given. In any case I put in a disappointing performance when I came to sit the Common Entrance Exam for Eton, obtaining a strictly mediocre Middle Fourth grading when Upper Fourth was what had been expected of me.

But this was no disappointment as far as my father or my mother were concerned. It should be recalled that Henry himself had failed for Eton completely, while Daphne had never survived the course at any of the schools she had attended. Although I was aware, personally, that I should have done better, as far as my family were concerned it was deemed that I was doing all right.

# Chapter 23

## Sex: Further homosexual development

Before turning my attention to my homosexual development over this period, I'll take a look at my emergent (if suppressed) heterosexual tendencies.
For in retrospect, I am inclined to judge that I had been truly smitten with
a love for my cousin Sally-Anne Vivian.

I shall try to analyse this in greater depth.

The opportunities for developing my relationship with Sal had largely
been lacking. But I remembered with emotion the way she had once mean-
ingfully told me that I was her favourite cousin, and it seemed to me that
in all probability this stated affinity between the two of us would inevitably
flower into something more colourful yet – without even excluding the
possibility of marriage. It was several years since we had expressed a particular liking for one another, and there was no real way of knowing if she still
felt the same way towards myself as I felt towards her.

I had taken the unwise step of confiding some element of my sentimental feelings towards Sal to my friend Wiggy, during that term. I had
said that I regarded this cousin to be my girl-friend, and had described to
him what she was like. Perhaps one should never trust any emotional confidence to a 'chief chum' in schooldays, but I had done so on this occasion,
and I lived to regret it in that he slipped the information to those in the
school who relished the opportunity of poking fun at such an idea. And it
might be said that there was considerable entertainment in the observation
of me blushing to a deep beetroot colour whenever the name of Sally-Anne
was maliciously thrown in my direction.

In one way or another – and I suspect Caroline on this occasion – the information that I regarded myself as enamoured with Sal then reached my parents. In Henry's eyes this was a huge joke. The very idea that I might have tender feelings for his niece was in some way regarded as a precocious absurdity. But there was an element of sadism too in his mirth – an idea that he was surrounded, in his pre-eminence, with lesser individuals who squirmed uncomfortably as he manipulated the manner in which values should be read from above their heads. It was not a question of whether he was right or wrong in such manipulation. It was an expression of his established superiority, which permitted him to praise or ridicule as he saw fit.

The setting was usually the dining-room at Sturford. The teasing about Sal would begin, and then Daphne would cry out: 'Oh, the poor darling! He's blushing again!' And there was Henry roaring with laughter, and my siblings smirking in deference to my father's mirth. No one seemed to appreciate that my feelings were precarious in this direction. I felt the need to cover them up, if not to obliterate them completely.

So I shall now turn to my less inhibited development within the homosexual arena. Not that such practices were ever encouraged by Ali Barber, but during this period of the war years, when the communal morale had been severely shaken by the enlistment of so many teachers upon whom the school ethos had formerly depended, it could be said that a spirit of degeneracy had arisen. Ali had called the school together on more than one occasion to lecture us, awkwardly, upon 'these lamentable games where one boy attempts to seize another boy by his private parts'. We were told that all such miscreants were 'loony fellows', but he never took the criticism much further than that.

We had all indulged in these games only marginally less than the generation a year or two older than ourselves, and under the tuition of [A] I had indulged in homosexual play in an ineffectual attempt to achieve orgasm. None of this involved a sentimental relationship to compare with what I felt for Sal, but it was less inhibited in that the current school ethos permitted such horseplay, inasmuch that it involved a healthy degree of disobedience to authority. There was no expression of disapproval for such practices within my immediate peer group, although I had always realised it was best to be discreet in the revelation of this side to my nature.

Let me now add to this a strain in homosexual development which derived specifically from Henry himself. On returning to Britain from Africa he had been concerned to tidy up my sloppy appearance, and to improve upon the general standard of my cleanliness. (He always did maintain that Nanny Marks, despite all her acknowledged virtues, had permitted a certain working-class squalor to reveal itself within the upbringing of his children.) His sons, but not his daughter – because she was the mother's concern – were now required to display to him their hands for inspection before a meal, with particular notice taken of whether we had properly scrubbed the dirt from beneath our fingernails. The hair also had to be well groomed during the holidays, smarmed into place with Brylcreem – until one of his friends from Whites' club suggested that this particular brand was only popular with the lower classes, whereupon the prescribed lotion changed to that of Honey & Flowers, which was purveyed by one of the hairdressing salons able to boast that they functioned by appointment to the royal family.

In his younger days, people might almost have described Henry as being 'a very pretty man' – a description that had indeed been applied to our ancestor, the 1st Marquess. This might underscore an essential effeminacy of physical appearance, without the accompaniment of feminine mannerisms. But I may have found it difficult as a boy to read correctly all that was being advocated to me in the expression of an appropriate image. I wished fervently to follow in my father's footsteps, and to become the sort of person who would merit his admiration and praise. The elements of sartorial vanity I was now picking up, however, were not altogether what my parents were intending, being more closely identified with what they scoffed at as 'pansy'. I was finding it hard to distinguish where the borderline of such behaviour might be drawn.

For example, I imagined incorrectly that I was assuming something of Henry's inherent elegance when I picked up the mannerism of cocking my little finger upwards when holding a cup of tea. (The idea had been suggested, humorously, by a conjuror when invited to perform at Ludgrove – poking fun, as I now see it, at the elitist cult within his audience.) My concern to participate within the school's extra-curricular dancing classes – with some degree of excellence, it might be added – also gave rise to teasing comment from some observers, including Cabbage Reed, and despite the fact that he regarded the spectacle of boys dancing with boys as in the best paedophile tradition of ancient Greece. And now that we stayed quite regularly at Claridges Hotel, both at the beginning and the end of our holidays, it was Henry himself who arranged for me to sit beside him in their gentlemen's hairdressing salon receiving a full-scale manicure of my fingernails.

The fun and games element in my homosexual development increased apace during my first term as a dormitory monitor, in which capacity the general tone of conduct was set by myself. Having kept those under me on a short leash, restraining their inclinations towards nocturnal games with the promise of full licence during the final week of the term, if only they would behave themselves prior to that, I fulfilled my side of the bargain by orchestrating an orgiastic scenario when their time finally arrived. I proclaimed marriages between different members of the dormitory, and we spent the entire week (or the nights thereof) practising what we assumed might be marital techniques in copulation. To the best of my knowledge, none of us achieved any orgasm, but this release from a former spirit of restraint was enjoyed by most of us, if not by all.

Then during the summer holidays of 1944 I was invited by [G], a boy slightly younger than myself, to come and stay with him to participate in a local cricket match, where one of the teams would include a large contingent of Ludgrovians. I had always liked [G]. We were regarded as the school's best dancers, for which reason if for no other we frequently selected one another as partners: myself as the male, and he as the female. But when it came to the question of sexual initiation, within that bedroom we shared in his house, he was certainly the more experienced of the two of us. I found myself participating in practices which I had never done before ... and quite frankly, enjoying them.

We experienced the indignity of getting caught in the act – by [F], who was not himself at Ludgrove, but who was to become an acquaintance later at Eton. He entered [G]'s bedroom without warning, and found us curled up in a heap together. His surprise was greater than our own, however, and the cultural climate which the house might purvey was something for [G] himself to set. [F] was full of apologies, initially, and then did his utmost to make us believe that things like this happened also at his own school. It might then have appeared that the values which we ourselves held represented the position of the majority. But I was to become aware later, at Eton, that this episode (amongst others I dare say) served to fuel the conviction in some quarters that I was of a predominantly homosexual disposition.

Once I had reached my thirteenth birthday, Henry performed what had probably been a family tradition since the days of the 1st Marquess, and suggested that we go for a walk in the woods together, ostensibly to shoot rabbits but in reality to deliver to me his official version of the facts of life. There was an awkward lull in our conversation while we were theoretically searching for rabbits, which were reluctant to display themselves, and I had a shrewd idea of the motivation for his invitation long before the lecture was actually delivered. Once we were comfortably seated upon a felled tree up in King's Bottom (an appropriately-named plantation on the

Longleat estate), he imparted to me some of his paternal wisdom.

He discovered, in what must have struck him as an anticlimax, that I had heard it all before. Now that he had got this far, however, he decided to proceed with his instruction – just in case I had got some of the detail confused. I learnt, for example, just how lucky I was that he'd had me circumcised as a baby. I would be protected from syphilis that way. Circumcised cocks were cleaner all round. Germs didn't linger in the foreskin. So I would never have to suffer the indignity of such an operation, as an adult, if I neglected to wash between my legs when out on safari in outlandish regions of the globe.

'It happened to a sergeant in the Wiltshire Yeomanry when we were out in the desert, and his old man was in the most awful state by the time we got him into hospital.'

Henry also expressed his astonishment that the word 'fuck' was already used in our smut talk at Ludgrove. 'Nobody would have known that word in my schooldays.'

Apparently his mother had taken upon herself the task of instructing him about what one should and should not do in sexual behaviour.

'She'd got it all wrong, you know. They thought in those days that masturbation would drive you insane. She told me that people who abused themselves ended up in a lunatic asylum. And she had me scared stiff that this was going to happen to me. But you needn't worry. I can assure you that it does nothing of the kind ... I don't care what else you do, but I expressly forbid you to bugger anyone. Buggery is disgusting. A filthy habit. It was something we picked up from the Bulgarians, I'm told – during one of the wars in that part of the world.'

When I got back to Ludgrove for my final summer term, I discovered that my sex talk with Henry stimulated much interest within the conversations which took place in the monitors' bathroom – a select and relatively private room for our privileged ablutions. We had known already about commonplace copulation, but the information on buggery was new to us. And the very fact of knowing about it tickled our curiosity. A particular friend and myself during these final terms were perhaps more adventurous than the others in experimenting to see if such indecency was in fact physically possible. But we didn't take it any further than that.

In contrast to the sex instruction which I had received from Henry, Ali Barber had his own contribution to make. His confidential chats with those boys who were on the brink of departure from the school were invariably anticipated with a fair amount of juvenile mirth. When my own turn came, he warned me that I might find myself, quite soon, with a painful feeling in my private parts.

'Painful?' I queried.

He gave me one of his long and languid looks.

'Has it already happened to you?' he eventually enquired.

'I think so, sir,' I replied in all solemnity, without wishing to reveal that any actual orgasm was still unattainable, as far as I was concerned.

Long and languidly he gave the matter some further thought before finally stating: 'When you feel like that, it's probably best if you leave your private parts alone.' He didn't take the subject any further than that.

I indulged in one final homosexual weekend fling while I was at Ludgrove, and this was during the scouts' camp at Barewood. [D], whom I had previously instructed on how to masturbate, was now in my Badgers' patrol, and at his suggestion I invited him to share my tent with me. It could be that he felt quite sentimentally about his former sexual initiation, but in any case I enjoyed it too. We had quite a romp together, under the averted supervision of our homosexual scoutmaster.

Reverting to the subject of my heterosexual development, it should perhaps be noted that there had been far more freedom to develop in that other field. The very mention of Sally-Anne was enough to stir me into agonies of blushing, whereas the fun and games in homosexual intercourse went unchallenged – except inasmuch that there was a recognised risk attached to the commendable activity of flouting the dictates of those in authority. I accepted that women were to be regarded as a species apart, and that the true gentleman does nothing to upset their psychology. But it was my uncertainty as to what this psychology comprised that rendered me so vulnerable.

I knew my mother and my sister very well, of course. Even so, the idea had been instilled in my brain that I should defer to their wishes, notwithstanding my own. How should I know what other women might want? I had no confidence in how I should approach them. But I was relatively at ease with this my peer group of pubescent males.

# Chapter 24

## Authority: A foretaste of power

During the four years I had been at Ludgrove I had experienced phases of varying popularity. I had never been specifically unpopular, but there had been times when I had seemed to be swimming along with life better than at others. There had been a wave of popularity for me under the clowning image (as 'Twitter'), but it soon palled on those who wished to be more intent upon their studies – until I became aware of the hostility I had engendered.

As far as cliques within my peer group were concerned, the dominant personality within one of them was **[H]**. He was quiet, studious and relatively intellectual. Some of my friends were his friends, but there was never much of a liking between himself and me. There was only one period when I had endeavoured to associate closely with his clique, when he was creating a puppet theatre group. Then I soon found myself at odds with him – for reasons I shall attempt to analyse.

It probably boils down to the idea that I didn't know my place. It was **[H]** who had set up the theatre, devised the scripts and the characterisation, and here was I (admitted to the group for the sole reason that we happened to share a mutual friend) attempting to assert my own personality as if it were important. I dare say that **[H]** would have added that my contributions were disruptive and untalented. In any case, there came a point in time when he sent me a curt note, by the hand of another member of the group, which read quite simply: 'YOU'RE SACKED!' And I felt bitterly offended, for I did not then comprehend why it was that I should be regarded as unacceptable within their gang.

I recovered from this period of rejection in my own way, and partly because I was becoming the nucleus of a different gang of friends, which included Anthony Casdagli, Mark Jeffreys and Mark Dent-Brocklehurst, and partly because I had maintained almost constantly, the esteem of Ali Barber, who began promoting me to positions of authority above their heads. He made me aware that he regarded me as someone who displayed leadership qualities. He was always addressing the school on the need for such qualities, and perhaps I had been more attentive to his words than the rest of them.

Indeed, I always strove to emerge within the spirit of what he was preaching, offering the initial suggestion or example that he might demand. I had noted on a whole variety of occasions that he threw a glance of approval in my direction on observing that it was myself, rather than than those senior to me, who volunteered such a response. Leadership was one of the qualities most admired by my father as well. I knew how I might be pleasing the two of them with this display.

I was first appointed to be a dormitory monitor for the summer term of 1944. Ali had probably made it his business to ensure that I had a list of amiable boys to control, without any particular trouble-makers numbered in their ranks. I certainly had an easy run over the course of the term, persuading them to be on their best behaviour over the course of the entire term, with promises of jam tomorrow – or in the final week of term. (A promise that was fulfilled in the orgiastic scenes previously described.)

But Ali was evidently so impressed by my control over the dormitory during the initial weeks of the term that he elevated my status to that of school monitor, during that same term, and some while before my seniority as a dormitory monitor required. And it was this promotion which in fact gave me the edge over other candidates for the ultimate appointment as the captain of the school during my final term of summer 1945.

It was a case of attaining the pinnacle of power which had been many a schoolboy's secret ambition from the very start. I had never been a front runner for such distinction – until after my appointment as a school monitor, that is to say. But the whole idea of leadership qualities had been so much instilled into my vision as the desirable direction for personal development, both by Mr Barber and by my father himself, that the urge had always been present to earn their admiration by such achievement. And now that I had emerged as the leader, so to speak, I was determined to prove myself the best captain of the school that there had ever been.

This is where all that recent fascist indoctrination from Henry bore fruit. And a very sour fruit it turned out to be.

His precept for the archetypal leader was strength – in the sense of a capacity to dominate all others so that the decisions of his will were what counted in the direction that the group should take. So in accordance with this philosophy I endeavoured to instil into the minds of the other monitors the importance of our emerging in the eyes of the school as an integrated leadership, whose authority would unquestioningly be obeyed.

At the start, I dare say that the morale was good. I launched myself with verve into the duty of organising rosters and schedules, and seeing that the tasks thus allocated were efficiently executed. There were murmurs of praise from such long-standing admirers as Cabbage Reed. And I was popular in the school at large, with a following of stalwart supporters just a little junior to myself, with Paddy Cleland, Geoffrey Shackerley, Nick Crossley and Colin Ingleby-Mackenzie perhaps foremost amongst these. I seemed to be heading for a confirmation in spirit that I was developing along the right lines, towards the attainment of adult glory.

As in all fascist regimes throughout history, the goodwill towards such authority eventually floundered. In part this was due to the unpopularity of my second-in-command, who was[I]. [I] was just marginally older than me, had in fact been appointed a school monitor at the same time as myself, and had risen indeed to be head boy, which is to say he was listed top, from the previous term, in scholastic matters. I got on very well with [I], ever since I had earned his respect in the boxing ring, and by my emergent eminence in the flowering of juvenile persona. But he had a reputation for being tough, even harsh, with those younger than himself, and Mr Barber had probably promoted me over the top of his head, perhaps for that very reason, in my appointment as captain of the school.

[I] had greeted with enthusiasm my stress upon the need for strong leadership from the school monitors. But the question remained as to how this policy should best be implemented. It seemed that we had found an appropriate opportunity to demonstrate the principles upon which we intended to act when it was reported to us that [J], a boy with a reputation for bullying those younger than himself, had been terrorising some of the new kids by imprisoning them for spells of half an hour or so in a drawer intended for rackets, inside the changing-room of the squash court.

Within the spirit of letting the punishment fit the crime, we decided to give [J] a taste of his own medicine. He was ambushed, dragged into the first division, where a trap-door which gave access to a shallow, dusty space beneath the floor had been opened up in readiness for his own imprisonment. He climbed in without demur, but then displayed sufficient ingenuity to escape, so that the whole process had to be repeated – with greater attention this time to the placement of something heavy on top of the trap-door. On this occasion the sentence was completed, and we congratulated ourselves upon what we regarded as the successful enforcement of law and order – by ourselves as the self-appointed vigilantes.

Incarceration in 'the priest-hole' (as it was called) had in fact been employed at Ludgrove, according to verbal tradition, by a particular set of monitors shortly prior to the time when we ourselves had first arrived at the school. The fear of incurring such a fate had remained imprinted upon our minds, to an extent that the threat of such punishment had long served as a deterrent against too much cheek from the junior boys towards those who had reached the first division. The fact that we were now putting such punishment into practice must sadly be regarded as the implementation of my own (or Henry's) precept that leadership should be strong.

And it seemed for a while that we had achieved what we desired, in that the more bumptious of those who were younger than us now curtailed their cheek, scuttling out of our way or behaving deferentially towards us, their dour looks held askance.

I think I am right in saying that it was [I] who argued, during this instant flush of success, that we ought to take the policy further. And there was one boy in particular, [K], whom he regarded as being obnoxious, and therefore meriting a spell of incarceration under the floorboards. So another ambush was arranged, and [K] submitted to the fate imposed. Much to [I]'s fury, however, a note was intercepted from the prisoner's best friend, [L], commiserating with him on the treatment he had received, with some offensive reference to [I] whom he apparently regarded as the instigator of these actions.

Such comment was regarded as unacceptable, and as one further case of cheek which merited deterrent punishment. [I] took it upon himself to seize the unfortunate [L] and started lashing him with a belt before the sentence of imprisonment was carried out. I had been sitting there at my desk in the first division, without actually participating in the scene. But [L] now tearfully appealed to me that I should call a halt to what was going on. He even said something to the effect that I was far too descent a person for him to believe that I had ever endorsed such behaviour.

Little did he perceive just how guilty I really was, but I was generally popular in the school, whereas [I] was feared. This appeal to my better nature, however, made me feel really bad. [L] had been in my dormitory on various occasions, and I rather liked him. The sight of him receiving those (admittedly few) lashes was shameful to me, and for the first time I was glimpsing the grim shadow cast by the policies I had initiated. I told [I] hastily that the lashes were unnecessary, but that the sentence of incarceration could be implemented.

In retrospective examination of my school career, I am naturally horrified by these events. But it is important that I should record precisely what was going on in my mind, for I genuinely believed that I was exemplifying in my behaviour the very best of leadership qualities, those that Henry himself had preached, and those that would earn his respect and admiration. This can indeed be seen in the tone of my letter informing him of all that we had done. It must have been written immediately after [K]'s imprisonment, and prior to that of [L].

I shall quote some excerpts.

> We seem to have a lot more power than the usual standard of monitors. We found out that a cheeky little brat named [J] was bullying the new kids ... Immediately, we laid an ambush for him, and when he came near the 1st Div door, we pounced upon him and dragged him inside. We opened up the floorboards and I threw him down ... We left him down there for over an hour ...
>
> This morning we tried it again, on another person, this time under the offence of being too big for his boots. As it wasn't nearly such a bad case, I merely kept him there for about 15 minutes.

A point to be noticed, perhaps, is that I quite evidently regarded myself to be the ringleader. And I was – even if I mitigate this judgement in retrospect by saying that the influence of [I] had augmented the brutality of all that we did.

What came as a grave shock to me, however, was Henry's letter in reply to my own. I have no record of it, but in it he stated that I had misbehaved – that what I proclaimed as strength was in fact bullying, and that he was going to bring these matters to the attention of Mr Barber.

> My **eag**er **fil**ial **ears filled** with the **blaz**ing
> **fasc**ist **catch-phras**es, expo**und**ed in **flow**
> at the **round tab**le where a **host's** pre**rog**ative pre**vailed**,
> **failed** to dis**cern** the **bars** which **jarred** against **life**.

194

> **Stif**ling the **aspi**rations of a **size**able **heart,**
> while **stand**ing un**cer**tain at **school**ing's **starting-gate,**
> **art**ful, I'd **el**bowed my **tell**ing **way** with **bomb**ast
> and a**plomb,** to **mer**it the **murk**y **hal**o of **dom**inance.
> **Prom**inent as you **taught,** I **thrust** their dis**gust**ing **ton**sils
> **down** the **bent pip**ing of their **impious throats.**
> Yet a **boast**ing **letter** pro**claim**ing my **prow**ess **met**
> your **wet threat** to ex**pose** me as a **bully** to the **Head.**
> This earthquake tremor sent a warning shrill
> to torpid parts of me which trusted – still.

Psychologically, I had indeed been shaken. In supposing that I had been performing thus for Henry's benefit, I imagined that I had been sharing with him some manner of spiritual *entente*. I might turn out to be the personal fulfilment of all that he had been preaching. But I was now being told that I had somehow interpreted his preaching wrongly, and I was suddenly, despairingly, on my own. Was it really I who had erred so grossly in the reading of his word? Or was it he who didn't truly comprehend the significance of his own utterances?

But in any case I was now on my own, to sort out within my own values the kind of person that I should be.

The truth of the matter is that there was indeed an exceptionally strong streak of traditional public-school decency within my mental outlook. Mr Barber certainly, and my father in part at least, had conditioned me that way. It was all in the ethic of becoming a gentleman. The worry which had awakened in my mind, however, was that Henry didn't himself know how gentlemanly and fascist behaviour might logically be disassociated.

I have no means of knowing for sure whether it was Henry or one of our victims who informed Ali Barber about what had been going on. By my own deduction, he was probably informed from both sources. I think that my father must have written, because Ali quite evidently found himself under commitment to deal leniently with us. And I think that [L] had (quite rightly) informed on us, because Ali had been given the impression that [I], rather than myself, was the real culprit.

All of the school monitors were interviewed, both separately and collectively, to unearth the details of what exactly had occurred. At the end of the day, Ali admonished us for being 'the weakest set of monitors that Ludgrove has ever known'. This was hitting me, astutely, where it really hurt. But he didn't remove me from the captaincy of the school, and it felt at the time as if we all recovered with some resilience from the stigma of such shame.

I certainly enjoyed this my last term at Ludgrove – all of the four years I had spent there, in effect. Despite the final notoriety, I had in fact gained enormously in self-confidence over this period in my life. It had furnished me with a first taste of success. Even if I knew that I hadn't quite understood as yet what leadership qualities might really entail, it couldn't be denied that, somehow or other, I had come out on top. Whatever the necessary qualities might be, I felt that in essence I must possess them.

# Chapter 25

## Identity: A colourful hothouse plant

The time has come to review the nature of this boy, who was so eager to persuade himself that he had climbed already to the top of the slippery pole, in terms of success at his preparatory school, in readiness for his next phase of education at the illustrious Eton College.

And I must admit that in retrospect I have mixed feelings as to what he was really like.

If my contemporary school reports were to be lumped together as a whole, they would not portray the image of a specially gifted pupil. 'Always tries hard ... painstakingly slow, and it takes him time to grasp new ideas ... full of enthusiasm which is sometimes misplaced ... apt to take himself too seriously, and he is inclined to become agitated under pressure ... has a plentiful store of good sense ... has been a valuable influence in the school, and we like his open friendly nature.' My school reports for art were consistently good, incidentally, even though the importance attached to it at Ludgrove was minimal. The one I received after my final term reads: 'Both he and his brother are quite outstanding for natural genius in this subject, and should go far.'

I had enjoyed a considerable amount of popularity in the school at large, which had managed to survive the initial notoriety of my reign as captain of the school. On the other hand it would be a mistake for me to gloss over those events as being matters of little significance. There is quite a strain of bullying behaviour discernible, as I endeavoured to emerge as the personification of true leadership values such as Henry had preached them to be – all of this in my efforts to secure myself in a position of authority during my final year at Ludgrove. In the dormitory I had often relied on the penalty of swishing (beating) with a slipper those who had transgressed my rules.

The worst case that I can remember consisted of my instructing the others in my dormitory, during my final term, to tie **[M]** to his bed. He was then my second-in-command in Dorm 10, and someone that I counted as a friend. But he was always insubordinate and generally difficult to handle, so I must have judged that he merited such discipline. The assembled company then threw slippers at his spreadeagled form, until his tears revealed that he was suitably contrite. Indeed, such treatment of offenders was then quite commonplace at Ludgrove.

All of this needs to be judged against the contrasting vein of public-school decency which also prevailed – by which I mean values such as are extolled in Rudyard Kipling's or in Hugh Walpole's tales about school life. Indeed, I have my own memory of admonishing with silent frown the new kid suffering from home-sickness whom I saw weeping silently in his bed – thus saving him from the jeering ridicule of the rest of the dormitory, who would have been quick to persecute such an evident display of emotional vulnerability. Despite all that bullying streak within my recent development, the thoroughly decent good sort of chap was still there, firmly ingrained. Essentially, I was a really nice guy – but a trifle confused about the directions for the development that was expected of me.

Something of which I feel more critical in retrospect was the element of falsity in the presentation of my affections. For example, Miss Vigers came down to see me at Ludgrove during my final term, and I reverted instantly to the attitude of affectionate regard which she expected of me. My arm slid all too easily into hers, and I was calling her 'Vigey', at her request – in mendacious affirmation of a closeness in spirit which she erroneously recalled.

Henry had indeed preached such tactics as desirable. I can remember him smiling with full charm and admitting at the most to a cynicism towards all those 'soft-soap' values which we put up front to obtain what we need to obtain from life. But to get 'sucked in' by such values was to be taken as a sign of weakness: something for women, and strictly not for men – unless they were effeminate.

It wasn't just with Miss Vigers that I found myself behaving thus. During the latter stage of the war, Mrs Corrigan (my American godmother) had returned to the London scene. She had been sending me cheques for £10 regularly at birthday and Christmas ever since I could truly remember. And the need to keep in good favour with her had always been stressed by both of my parents. It had, after all, been the basis of their own good relationship with her. Now that she was back in London, she had rented an entire suite of rooms at Claridges Hotel, to which we were all sometimes invited for a meal.

Her attitude towards me was somewhat embarrassing. I was invariably seated next to her at the luncheon-table, and putting her arms round my neck, she would say things like: 'Now tell me, which is your favourite auntie?'

I had never even regarded her as one of my aunts, prior to that moment, but the reply was instantly on my lips. 'It's Aunt Laura!'

Such cupboard-love was expected of me by all parties concerned. And the requirement to seem all-embracingly affectionate was carried to the point of eating the occasional cooked oyster extended in my direction, skewered upon a fork that had already been used to feed herself. This conflicted grossly with my conditioning against having the traces of any other person's saliva touching my own tongue. But a hasty examination of the expressions on my parents' faces dictated where my priorities in conditioning should lie.

I find it interesting in retrospect to remember how Henry was quite critical of Aunt Laura behind her back. There was the very question of putting cooked oysters on the menu, for example. This was evidence of dubious class origins, in his book, since people who really knew how to behave in high society would always offer oysters to be eaten raw, with a squeeze of lemon. I suspect personally that Laura ordered cooked oysters because there were children present – and I must admit to a secret craving for that delicacy, which I have never since had the good fortune to find on offer.

There was another incident at this same luncheon, when Henry was teasing Laura about her figure, to which she indignantly retorted: 'I'll have you know that my figure was the pride of Paris. My breasts are as round and as rosy as apples.' This remark gave rise, later, to his comment that she really didn't know where to stop, when it came to blowing her own trumpet. There should be finesse in everything – if one was going to try to live by upper-class standards.

But I should focus, perhaps, upon the idea of perceiving my identity at this particular moment in time, in relation to all that had been going on around me. These were the final months of the war. The VE (Victory in Europe) celebrations took place during my final summer term at Ludgrove. It was all fairly subdued because our school comprised a relatively isolated community. But we all joined in the festive spirit of national euphoria, building a large bonfire around which we all sang songs late into the evening.

And the VJ (Victory in Japan) celebrations fell during the summer holidays, when we were up in Anglesey staying with our Stanley cousins.

Henry had in fact rejoined the family on extended leave (virtually demobilised, because he wasn't by any means an essential member of General Pete Corlett's staff) several months prior to the cessation of hostilities. So we were all up in Anglesey at the time of these VJ celebrations. The cousins were ardent yachtsmen, and we all went mackerel fishing. Then came the moment when someone had to degut the fish, and it was noted by Henry how it was myself, rather than Christopher, who performed the task without demur, and unsqueamishly – well trained by Tom Renyard, of course.

He said reprovingly to Chris: 'I always thought you were the more manly of the two!'

My glory was short-lived.

We all went down to the fair in Holyhead that evening, where I found myself sharing a swing-boat with my cousin Richard. Then I began to feel sick. But Henry was in the boat next to ours, swinging ever higher in the company of Chris, so I delayed my cry for help to the fairground attendant for just too long. The man then ran to raise the board which, when lifted, arrests the pendulum motion of these swing boats, but he suffered the penalty of arriving underneath just at the moment when I could no longer restrain my vomit.

It wasn't the most glorious of postures in which to remember myself at this the end of the Second World War. There was even a certain lack of sympathy for my predicament, accentuated by an inner knowledge that I hadn't quite matched up to the expectations for me, and that despite my recent manliness in drawing the guts from all those dead mackerel, Chris had now turned the tables on me, once again, to earn Henry's esteem. It was an image of me which somehow epitomised my situation at this moment when global hostilities were finally concluded.

I was to understand in retrospect how the war years represented a complete gulf between two different eras – even if it took me a long time subsequently to work out my relationship with the new society that I was in the process of entering. The war itself had left me both physically, and psychologically intact. Friends of my parents, but no relatives, had actually been killed. The front line had always been far distant. But like everyone else, if individually in my own special way, I had learnt something about fascism and all that it stood for.

I had evolved quite rapidly through various stages in my relationship towards such ideas. I had perceived their attraction, even attempting to put them into practice. But I had also experienced disgrace in such self-proclaimed elitism – a disposition more akin perhaps to an attitude to be found in nations that had suffered occupation by, and participated in collaboration with, the Nazi regime.

This endowed some character to what was, after all, a highly personal experience of the Second World War. I might well feel that I had been disillusioned with fascism but I still needed to ask myself what the alternative to the fascists' solution for the world might be. If people were left to themselves to exercise democracy as they saw fit, they had shown us that they elect a Labour government. And these Socialists – according to Henry, in any case – were anathema to our own aristocratic style of living.

If I had recently acquired an uncertainty with regard to fascism, I most certainly held doubts about the efficacy of democracy.

This was the world in which I found myself, however, and I vaguely realised that a choice in direction must sometime finally be made.

*to be continued*